The American Psyche

Black and White

By S.J. Claybon

ISBN:
979-8-9881989-0-1 - eBook
979-8-9881989-1-8 - Paperback
979-8-9881989-2-5 - Hardcover

Published by
Amazon Publishing Agency

Table of Contents

Dedication

To my Beloved Daughter Samantha Elise Claybon,

and in memory of my late parents,

Rosie Lee Walker Claybon, and Arthur Claybon Jr.

Acknowledgments

This book is the culmination of intensive research aimed at articulating the evolution of the American psyche since the genesis of the United States. The assembly of pertinent facts and figures required a herculean effort to validate the thesis I've endeavored to communicate to my readers. It was during the isolating period of the COVID-19 pandemic that my ideas for this book solidified, enabling me to establish a consistent routine to realize this venture.

This work attempts to demystify the intricate mindset of the American populace. It aspires to illuminate the psychological underpinnings that sustain and perpetuate racism in the United States, thus deepening our comprehension of its broad societal ramifications.

My heartfelt thanks go to Winslow, Solomon, Dawn, Billie, Frank, and Michelle, whose steadfast support and encouragement were pivotal throughout this literary journey. Also, I express infinite gratitude for the COVID-19 pandemic that accorded me the solitude to realize my vision to this book's completion.

Chapter 1
Shaping the Psyche of the American People

Two critical documents shaped the foundation of this Nation: The Declaration of Independence and The United States Constitution. These two documents set the precedent for ushering in a wave of anti-Black policies, laws/statutes, and devastating Supreme Court case decisions that shaped the American Psyche.

On July 4, 1776, the Second Continental Congress met in Philadelphia, Pennsylvania, and adopted the United States Declaration of Independence. The Declaration of Independence, enacted during the American Revolution, explains why the Thirteen Colonies at war with the United Kingdom of Great Britain saw themselves as thirteen independent sovereign republics no longer under British dominion. With the Declaration of Independence, these new colonies took a collective first step toward becoming the United States of America.

Most of the population of the thirteen colonies were Protestant Christians, liberating themselves from the oppressive rule of the Britain Monarchy. This was a great opportunity in history to embrace all humanity and show the world that the newly independent United States would live up to the great words:

"We hold these truths to be self-evident, that all men are created equal, that they are endowed by their Creator with certain unalienable rights, that among these are Life, Liberty and the pursuit of Happiness."[1]

---

[1] *Declaration of Independence (1776) - Bill of Rights Institute*. (n.d.). Bill of Rights Institute. https://billofrightsinstitute.org/primary-sources/declaration-of-independence

Despite the unjust treatment from the British Monarchy and the beautiful words "*all men are created equal, that they are endowed by their Creator with certain unalienable rights,*" these same people were holding men, women, and children in bondage, preserving one of the most sinister, brutal, and dehumanizing chattel slavery systems known to man. This was all based on a white supremacy system used to control the lives of human beings for profit, power, greed, hatred, racism, and free labor.

The Constitution of the United States is the "supreme law of the land." The national government framework is defined in this foundational Constitution, which initially consisted of seven articles.

The first three articles enshrine the doctrine of separation of powers, which divides the federal government into three branches: (Article I); legislative Powers, which include the bodies of Congress (Senate and House of Representatives). (Article II); executive powers, which include the (President and Vice-President) and (Article III); judicial powers, which include the (Supreme Court and other federal courts).

Articles IV, V, and VI describe state governments' rights and obligations, the state's relationship to the federal government, and the collaborative process of a constitutional amendment. Article VII outlines the procedure for the original thirteen states to ratify the treaty.

In 1788, the United States Constitution was ratified, making it the legal structure of the country's governance.

Constitution Preamble: *"We the People of the United States, in order to form a more perfect Union, establish Justice, ensure domestic Tranquility, provide for the common defense, promote the general Welfare, and secure the Blessing of Liberty to ourselves and our Posterity, do ordain and establish this Constitution for the United States of America."[2]*

The framers of the Constitution were deliberate in their writing; the document implied slavery and the slave trade without literally mentioning the words in the document. They used the words "(Person," "Persons," or "other Persons)" to indicate slavery/slave trade. James Madison, known as the father of the U.S. Constitution and the 4th President of the United States, stated at the 1787 Constitutional Convention that *"it was wrong to admit in the Constitution about the idea that there could be property in men."[3]* This was a clear indication that the framers recognized that enslaving human beings was morally wrong but consciously refused to correct that moral wrong.

Article 1, Section 9, Clause 1

"The Migration or Importation of such Persons as any of the States now existing shall think proper to admit, shall not be prohibited by the Congress before the Year one thousand eight hundred and

---

[2] *U.S. Senate: Constitution of the United States. (2021d, July 21). https://www.senate.gov/civics/constitution_item/constitution.htm#preamble*

[3] Spies-Gans, Paris A. (2017). "James Madison". *The Princeton & Slavery Project. https://slavery.princeton.edu/stories/james-madison.*

eight, but a Tax or duty may be imposed on such Importation, not exceeding ten dollars for each Person."[4]

This prohibited the federal government from banning the importation of "African Slaves" until the year (1808), twenty years after the ratification of the U.S. constitution.

In the sixth annual message to Congress on December 2, 1806, this is what President Thomas Jefferson spoke about the impending expiration of (Article 1, Section 9, Clause 1).

"I congratulate you, fellow citizens, on the approach of the period at which you may interpose your authority constitutionally to withdraw the citizens of the United States from all further participation in those violations of human rights which have been so long continued on the unoffending inhabitants of Africa, and which the morality, the reputation, and the best interests of our country, have long been eager to proscribe. Although no law you may pass can take prohibitory effect till the first day of the year one thousand eight hundred and eight. Yet, the intervening period is not too long to prevent, by timely notice, expeditions which cannot be completed before that day."[5]

Article 1, Section 2, Clause 3

"Representatives and direct Taxes shall be apportioned among the several States which may be included within this Union, according

---

[4] *U.S. Senate: Constitution of the United States.* (2021c, July 21). https://www.senate.gov/civics/constitution_item/constitution.htm#a1

[5] *Sixth Annual Message | The American Presidency Project.* (n.d.). https://www.presidency.ucsb.edu/documents/sixth-annual-message

to their respective Numbers, which shall be determined by adding to the whole Number of free <u>*Persons*</u>*, including those bound to Service for a Term of Years, and excluding Indians not taxed, three-fifths of all* <u>*other Persons*</u>*."[6]*

This states that "African Slaves' would be counted as "three-fifths" of a free individual (white citizen) to determine the number of congressional representations.

<u>*Article IV, Section 2, Clause 2*</u>

"No <u>*Person*</u> *held to Service or Labour in one State, under the Laws thereof, escaping into another, shall, in Consequence of any Law or Regulation therein, be discharged from such Service or Labour, but shall be delivered up on Claim of the Party to whom such Service or Labour may be due."[7]*

This is known as the "Fugitive Slave Clause," which states that if an "African Slave" escapes into another state, that state's individual must return the fugitive "African Slave" to the state from which the "African Slave" came.

Two years after the ratification of the U.S. Constitution, in 1790, Congress passed the Nationality Act, which limited U.S. citizenship to "whites" only immigrants, and "white" preferences remained until the 1965 Immigration and Nationality Act.

---

[6] *U.S. Senate: Constitution of the United States.* (2021c, July 21). https://www.senate.gov/civics/constitution_item/constitution.htm#a1

[7] *U.S. Senate: Constitution of the United States.* (2021c, July 21). https://www.senate.gov/civics/constitution_item/constitution.htm#a4

The Declaration of Independence references God and humanity in a paradoxical nature; however, the U.S. Constitution, *the supreme law of the land*, references neither. But every state's Constitution references God in some way! The debate that sparks from such references is about the role of God. What role does God play when people are divided into groups based on skin color? One group is privileged, and one group is despised. This has remained an unanswered question throughout history to date.

Most of the U.S. Presidents have been devoted Christians and sworn into office by putting their left hand on a Bible. Most politicians today mention God when grandstanding for political office, the "In God We Trust" symbol is printed on our currency, and we have churches clustered throughout every community in this country. As a nation, are we just anchored in this mystical relationship with God, yet refuse to admit the truth: white supremacy was foundational in building the governance/social structure of society, and is still a central theme to all our lives.

The U.S. Constitution aided in the reinforcement of shaping the inflated psyche of white Americans. It sanctioned their behavior and thoughts to perceive the enslaved Africans as less-than-human or objects. These people were dehumanized, tortured, mutilated, raped, shackled, denied education, and lynched, to name a few... This behavior could easily be described as psychopathic and was normalized using the law, essentially debasing, and vilifying enslaved Africans, all in the name of God.

For generations, whites were the only people allowed access to U.S. citizenship. Therefore, whites born and raised in this country and the newly received European immigrants were indoctrinated into the social structure of white supremacy, which promoted the dehumanization of human beings, and the dominant white culture normalized this behavior. This created an environment that defended this way of life, conducted research, authoring journals, articles, and books, attempting to prove that human beings could be divided into separate and exclusive biological entities and that white Anglo-Saxton were innately superior to others. Making their psychopathic behavior and treatment toward Black Americans righteous in the sight of God, resulting in generations of whites developing an inflated sense of self that persists to this day.

During this period, the United States created a litany of characters who would go on to perpetuate white supremacy behavior to the public and be awarded/recognized for their horrific acts. Here are a few examples:

Born in 1799 in Philadelphia, PA, Samuel George Morton was an American physician and writer. He published the book "Crania Americana" in 1839, about the comparative view of human skulls of North and South America in which he concluded that whites had superior intelligence because of the large size of their skulls.

James Marion Sims, born 1813 in Lancaster County, SC, was an American physician and the "Father of Gynecology" by repeatedly operating on enslaved Black women without anesthesia as though Black people could not feel pain only to perfect his surgical techniques. Could you imagine the excruciating pain and torture the many women endured?

Woodrow Wilson, born 1856 in Staunton, VA, was the 28th President of the United States (1913-1921), Nobel Peace Prize winner, 34th

Governor of New Jersey (1911-1913), and the 13th President of Princeton University (1902-1910). As President of the United States, he authorized segregation within the federal government, allowing agencies to adopt a white-only employment policy. He viewed the film "The Birth of a Nation" (one of the most racist films ever made) along with his family at the White House and stated, "It's like writing history with lightning. My only regret is that it is all so true".[8] This set the tone for anti-Black Hollywood media propaganda. I will delve further into this topic in an upcoming chapter.

Madison Grant, born in 1865 in New York City, was a lawyer/eugenicist who published the book "The Passing of the Great Race" in 1916. He claimed northern Europeans were biologically and culturally superior to the rest of humanity. The book played a significant role in formulating immigration and anti-miscegenation laws in the United States. Also, Adolf Hitler was a big fan of the book. He wrote to Grant, "The book is my Bible."

You may detect a recurring theme or pattern with these characters. These men were born after the ratification of the Constitution, they were educated professionals, intelligent but psychopathic, and arguably suffering from a narcissistic personality disorder. These deformed ways of being set the foundations for social ethics led by the leaders of this Nation. If the leaders, elite, and educated perpetuated this anti-Black behavior, how do you think it translated to the psyche of the working-class and poor/uneducated whites?

---

[8] Benbow, Mark E. "Birth of a Quotation: Woodrow Wilson and 'Like Writing History with Lightning.'" *The Journal of the Gilded Age and Progressive Era*, vol. 9, no. 4, 2010, pp. 509–33. *JSTOR*, http://www.jstor.org/stable/20799409.

White men created the social construct of race, and throughout the history of the United States, it has honored only a certain group of people and held them in high esteem. However, this great nation has never fully acknowledged that this country would not be the great nation it is without the resilient Black Americans who, despite enduring harsh circumstances throughout history, played an integral role in shaping the greatness of this country as it stands today. Under the United States Constitution, "the supreme law of the land," enslaved Black Americans were subjected to some of the most inhumane and dehumanizing treatment. But the United States government has never publicly recognized its significant role in building this nation without compensation.

Enslaved Black Americans were finally emancipated from chattel slavery in 1865, not because of moral considerations; instead, it was a result of the country being engaged in a war and the union's strategic motivations. So, President Abraham Lincoln issued the Emancipation Proclamation declaring "that all persons held as slaves within the rebellious Southern States are free." President Lincoln's statement:

"I would save the Union. I would save it the shortest way under the Constitution. If I could save the Union without freeing any slave, I would do it, and if I could save it by freeing all the slaves, I would do it; and if I could save it by freeing some and leaving others alone, I would also do that. I DO what I do about slavery and the colored race because I believe it helps save this Union".[9]

---

[9]*Letter to Horace Greeley (1862) | Lincoln's Writings.* (n.d.).
https://housedivided.dickinson.edu/sites/lincoln/letter-to-horace-greeley-august-22-1862/

During the Reconstruction era (1865-1877), though short-lived, Black Americans as a collective elected seven men to the U.S. Congress. Hiram Revels of Mississippi, U.S. Senator (1870-1871), Benjamin Turner of Alabama, U.S. House of Representatives (1871-1873), Jefferson Franklin Long of Georgia, U.S. House of Representatives (1871), Robert De Large of South Carolina, U.S. House of Representatives (1871-1873), Josiah Walls of Florida, U.S. House of Representatives (1871-1876), Joseph H. Rainey of South Carolina, U.S. House of Representatives (1870-1879), and Robert Brown Elliott of South Carolina, U.S. House of Representatives (1871-1874). There were many Blacks elected to city and state-level offices, even a Black governor (P.B.S. Pinchback) was appointed governor of Louisiana from (1872 to 1873).

Black Americans made great efforts to achieve and build thriving communities during and after the Reconstruction Era, even under extremely hostile conditions. However, out of pure hatred, white supremacist mobs would kill innocent people and burn down many of these communities. In the Colfax, Louisiana, massacre of (1873), over 150 Black men were murdered by white men with guns and cannons. Wilmington, North Carolina, in the massacre of (1889), over 300 Black people were murdered by a white mob. Atlanta, Georgia, in the massacre of (1906), over 100 Black people were murdered by 2000 white men. Elaine, Arkansas, in the massacre of (1919), over 200 Black people were murdered by a mob of white men. In the massacre of (1923), Rosewood, Florida, over 150 Black people were murdered by a white mob. In Tulsa, Oklahoma, during the massacre of (1921), over 300 Black people were murdered by a white mob.

Historical Landmark Supreme Court Cases: Civil Rights Case of 1883 and Plessy v. Ferguson

The 14[10] Amendment was ratified on July 9, 1868, and the Civil Rights Act of 1875 became law on March 1, 1875. Reading the 14th Amendment and Civil Rights of 1875 law below, there is no way you can misinterpret its intent or meaning.

14th Amendment:

SECTION 1.

All persons born or naturalized in the United States and subject to the jurisdiction thereof are citizens of the United States and the state they reside. No state shall make or enforce any law which shall abridge the privileges or immunities of citizens of the United States; nor shall any state deprive any person of life, liberty, or property, without due process of law; nor deny to any person within its jurisdiction the equal protection of the laws.[10]

Civil Rights Act of 1875

To protect all citizens in their civil and legal rights.

Whereas, it is essential to just government we recognize the equality of all men before the law, and hold that it is the duty of government in its dealings with the people to mete out equal and exact justice to all, of whatever nativity, race, color, or persuasion, religious or political; and it being the appropriate object of legislation to enact

---

[10] *U.S. Senate: Constitution of the United States.* (2021c, July 21).
https://www.senate.gov/civics/constitution_item/constitution.htm#a1

great fundamental principles into law: Therefore, Be it enacted by the Senate and House of Representatives of the United States of America in Congress assembled, That all persons within the jurisdiction of the United States shall be entitled to the full and equal enjoyment of the accommodations, advantages, facilities, and privileges of inns, public conveyances on land or water, theaters, and other places of public amusement; subject only to the conditions and limitations established by law, and applicable alike to citizens of every race and color, regardless of any previous condition of servitude.

__Sec. 2.__ That any person who shall violate the foregoing section by denying to any citizen, except for reasons by law applicable to citizens of every race and color, and regardless of any previous condition of servitude, the full enjoyment of any of the accommodations, advantages, facilities, or privileges in said section enumerated, or by aiding or inciting such denial, shall, for every such offense, forfeit and pay the sum of five hundred dollars to the person aggrieved thereby, to be recovered in an action of debt, with full costs; and shall also, for every such offense, be deemed guilty of a misdemeanor, and, upon conviction thereof, shall be fined not less than five hundred nor more than one thousand dollars, or shall be imprisoned not less than thirty days nor more than one year: Provided, That all persons may elect to sue for the penalty aforesaid or to proceed under their rights at common law and by State statutes; and having so elected to proceed in the one mode or the other, their right to proceed in the other jurisdiction shall be barred. But this proviso shall not apply to criminal proceedings, either under this act or the criminal law of any State: And provided further, that a judgment for the penalty in favor of the party *aggrieved, or a judgment upon an indictment, shall be a bar to either prosecution respectively.*

__Sec. 3.__ That the district and circuit courts of the United States shall have, exclusively of the courts of the several States, cognizance of all crimes and offenses against, and violations of, the provisions of this act; and actions for the penalty given by the preceding section may be prosecuted in the territorial, district, or circuit courts of the United States wherever the defendant may be found, without regard to the other party; and the district attorneys, marshals, and deputy marshals of the United States, and commissioners appointed by the circuit and territorial courts of the United States, with powers of arresting and imprisoning or bailing offenders against the laws of the United States, are hereby specially authorized and required to institute proceedings against every person who shall violate the provisions of this act, and cause him to be arrested and imprisoned or bailed, as the case may be, for trial before such court of the United States, or territorial court, as by law has cognizance of the offense, except in respect of the right of action accruing to the person aggrieved; and such district attorneys shall cause such proceedings to be prosecuted to their termination as in other cases: Provided, That nothing contained in this section shall be construed to deny or defeat any right of civil action accruing to any person, whether by reason of this act or otherwise; and any district attorney who shall willfully fail to institute and prosecute the proceedings herein required, shall, for every such offense, forfeit and pay the sum of five hundred dollars to the person aggrieved thereby, to be recovered by an action of debt, with full costs, and shall, on conviction thereof, be deemed guilty of a misdemeanor, and be fined not less than one thousand nor more than five thousand dollars: And *provided further, That a judgment for the penalty in favor or the party aggrieved against any such district attorney, or a judgment upon an indictment against any such district attorney, shall be a bar to either prosecution respectively.*

Sec. 4. That no citizen possessing all other qualifications which are or may be prescribed by law shall be disqualified for service as grand or petit juror in any court of the United States, or of any State, on account of race, color, or previous condition of servitude; and any officer or other person charged with any duty in the selection or summoning of jurors who shall exclude or fail to summon any citizen for the cause aforesaid shall, on conviction thereof, be deemed guilty of a misdemeanor, and be fined not more than five thousand dollars.

Sec. 5. That all cases arising under the provisions of this act in the courts of the United States shall be reviewable by the Supreme Court of the United States, without regard to the sum in controversy, under the same provisions and regulations as are now provided by law for the review of other causes in said court.[11]

After the passing of the Civil Rights Act of 1875, Black Americans continued to be discriminated against, and many filed discrimination cases in the courts. Five cases reached the Supreme Court (*U.S. Senate: Landmark Legislation: Civil Rights Act of 1875*). In 1883 the U.S. Supreme Court consolidated the five individual discrimination cases:

---

[11]*Civil Rights Act of 1875. The Supreme Court. The First Hundred Years. Primary Sources | PBS.* (n.d.-b).
https://www.thirteen.org/wnet/supremecourt/antebellum/sources_document7.html

- United States v. Stanley: Stanley denied a Black American U.S. citizen accommodation and privileges of an Inn or Hotel.
- United States v. Singleton: Singleton denied a Black American U.S. citizen accommodation in a Theatre known as the Grand Opera House in New York.
- United States v. Ryan: Ryan denied a Black American U.S. citizen a seat in the dress circle of the Maguire's Theatre in San Francisco.
- United States v. Nichols: Nichols denied a Black American U.S. citizen accommodation and privileges of an Inn or Hotel.
- Robinson & Wife v. Charleston Railroad Company: Both Black American U.S. citizens but the wife was not allowed to ride in the lady's car because she was Black American.

The consolidation of these five cases is known today as the historical "Civil Rights case of 1883". The Court ruled 8-1, declaring the Civil Rights Act of 1875 unconstitutional. The one Judge dissenting was Justice John Marshall Harlan. He wrote a 21-page dissent interpreting the Constitution and the law on why it was vital to withhold his dissent to the Court's opinion. Here is an excerpt of his closing statement of his dissent paper:

If the constitutional amendments be enforced according to the intent with which, as I conceive, they were adopted, there cannot be, in this republic, any class of human beings in practical subjection to another class with power in the latter to dole out to the former just such privileges as they may choose to grant. The supreme law of the land has decreed that no authority shall be exercised in this country upon the basis of discrimination, in respect of civil rights, against freemen and citizens because of their race, color, or previous condition of servitude. To that decree -- for the due enforcement of which, by appropriate legislation, Congress has been invested with express power -- everyone must bow, whatever may have been, or whatever now are, his individual views as to the wisdom or policy either of the recent changes in the fundamental law or of the legislation which has been enacted to give them effect. For the reasons stated, I feel constrained to withhold my assent to the opinion of the court. "[12]

In 1892, Homer Plessy, a Black American man of mixed race, boarded a train car in New Orleans that was deemed a white-only car. Plessy was accused of violating Louisiana's "Separate Car Act of 1890."

Homer Plessy took the case to the New Orleans court, where Judge John Howard Ferguson presided over the case and upheld that Plessy had violated the law. However, Plessy challenged Louisiana counts ruling, forcing the case to be heard by the U.S. Supreme Court to rule on the constitutionality of the segregation law.

In 1896 the Court ruled 7-1 that the Louisiana law did not violate the Fourteenth Amendment of the U.S. Constitution. Again, the one Judge dissenting was Justice John Marshall Harlan. Here is an excerpt from his dissent paper:

"The white race deems itself to be the dominant race in this country. And so it is, in prestige, in achievements, in education, in wealth, and in power. So, I doubt not, it will continue to be for all time, if it remains true to its great heritage, and holds fast to the

---

[12]*Civil Rights Cases, 109 U.S. 3 (1883). (Harlan, John, M. dissent opinion) from WESTLAW*

principles of constitutional liberty. But in view of the constitution, in the eye of the law, there is in this country no superior, dominant, ruling class of citizens. There is no caste here. Our constitution is colorblind, and neither knows nor tolerates classes among citizens."[13]

And here is an excerpt of his closing statement of his dissent paper:

"I am of the opinion that the state of Louisiana is inconsistent with the personal liberty of citizens, white and black, in that state, and hostile to both the spirit and letter of the constitution of the United States. If laws of like character should be enacted in the several states of the Union, the effect would be in the highest degree mischievous. Slavery, as an institution tolerated by law, would, it is true, have disappeared from our country; but there would remain a power in the states, by sinister legislation, to interfere with the full enjoyment of the blessings of freedom, to regulate civil rights, common to all citizens, upon the basis of race, and to place in a condition of legal inferiority a large body of American citizens, now constituting a part of the political community, called the 'People of the United States,' for whom, and by whom through representatives, our government is administered. Such a system is inconsistent with the guaranty given by the constitution to each state of a republican form of government, and may be stricken down by congressional action, or by the courts in the discharge of their solemn duty to maintain the supreme law of the

---

[13]*Plessy v. Ferguson, 163 U.S. 537 (1896). (Harlan, John, M. dissent opinion) from WESTLAW*

land, anything in the constitution or laws of any state to the contrary notwithstanding."

"For the reason stated, I am constrained to withhold my assent from the opinion and judgment of the majority."[14]

As I mentioned above, this was another great opportunity in history to embrace all humanity and show the world that the United States would live up to the great words:

"We hold these truths to be self-evident, that all men are created equal, that they are endowed by their Creator with certain unalienable rights, that among these are Life, Liberty and the pursuit of Happiness."[15]

However, the intentional subjective misinterpretation of the "Civil Rights Act of 1875" and the United States Constitution "14th Amendment" by the Supreme Court Justices denied Black Americans equal justice under the law. The ruling, in these cases, ultimately led to the enactment of the "Jim Crow Laws" and the "separate but equal law" in the Southern States, which solidified the bond of poor and wealthy whites to impose the social order of white supremacy aggressively. This was a tremendous setback for Black Americans, who were subjected to an onslaught of violence, disenfranchisement, exploitation, and death.

This pivotal moment in history further normalized the psychopathic behavior and anti-Black sentiments garnered by the

---

[14]*Plessy v. Ferguson, 163 U.S. 537 (1896). (Harlan, John, M. dissent opinion) from WESTLAW*

[15]Declaration of Independence (1776)." *Bill of Rights Institute*, 4 July 1776, billofrightsinstitute.org/primary-sources/declaration-of-independence.

greater white society. This sent a clear message that this way of being was valued at the highest level of the federal government. Civil rights and true justice for Black Americans were insignificant to them.

It took Congress eighty-one years later to pass the 1964 Civil Rights Act, after decades of civil rights protests and activism. The 1964 Civil Rights Act addressed issues such as discrimination based on religion, sex, national origin, race and color. The Act did not provide true equity for Black Americans, who were dehumanized, lynched, victimized, traumatized, marginalized, brutalized, and exploited for free & cheap labor.

Chattel slavery and the Jim Crow system were the foundation of the United States economy. At the time, the prosperity garnered in commerce, finance, and manufacturing was a direct result of free and cheap Black American labor, and Black Americans did not have the opportunity to participate and build individual wealth in that economy. This is the primary cause of the significant wealth disparity between white Americans and Black Americans in the present day.

Today you will often hear an American politician use "America's Original Sin" to reconcile with the past. However, it can be tricky when used by American politicians in discourse. If not carefully unpackaged, it can be falsely equated to "only chattel slavery" that occurred in some distant past. Within its racist bag of dirty laundry called "America's Original Sin," one will find a plethora of anti-Black laws and policies such as Jim Crow, housing, education, and criminal justice, to name a few. Designed to give whites non-competitive economic advantages in this country.

That is why I am always perplexed whenever I hear today's politicians reference the phrase "America's Original Sin," alluding to only the sins of chattel slavery and not the plethora of anti-Black de facto and de Jure laws/policies enacted after the emancipation. For example, in 2019, Senate Majority Leader Mitch McConnell, born 1947, in Sheffield, Alabama, in the heart of the Jim Crow era, was asked about the federal government paying reparations for slavery.

He stated, *"None of us currently living are responsible"* for *"America's Original Sin." "I don't think reparations for something that happened 150 years ago is a good idea for whom none of us currently living are responsible. We have tried to deal with our original sin of slavery by fighting a civil war, passing landmark civil rights legislation as we elected an African American president."*[16]

The question should have been about the federal government paying reparations for chattel slavery, the devastating historical anti-Black Supreme Court cases subjective decisions, the plethora of anti- Black laws and policies such as Jim Crow, housing, education, and criminal justice that have marginalized the Black community since the ratification of the *Supreme Law of The Land.*

---

[16]Sonmez, Felicia. (2019). McConnell says he's against reparations for slavery: 'It would be pretty hard to figure out who to compensate.' *Washington Post.*
https://www.washingtonpost.com/politics/mcconnell-says-hes-against-reparations-for-slavery-it-would-be-pretty-hard-to-figure-out-who-to-compensate/2019/06/18/9602330c-9205-11e9-b58a-a6a9afaa0e3e_story.html

As mentioned above, the framers were deliberate when they wrote the U.S. Constitution, "The Supreme Law of the Land." The document was steeped in anti-Blackness, which shaped the Psyche of American society. This gave white people a superiority complex toward Black Americans, leading to many anti-Black laws/policies and Supreme Court case decisions.

The U.S. Constitution, which still shapes and guides our lives today, has only been updated 27 times since its ratification in 1788 but has yet to produce racial equity for Black Americans.

See the updates in the table below:[17]

Amendment	Ratified	Description
1st	1791	Rights to Religion, Speech, Press, Assembly, Petition
2nd	1791	Right to Bear Arms
3rd	1791	Quartering of Soldiers
4th	1791	Search and Seizure
5th	1791	Grand Jury, Double Jeopardy, Self-Incrimination, Due Process
6th	1791	Rights of Accused in Criminal Prosecutions: Rights to Jury Trial, to Confront Opposing Witnesses, and to Counsel
7th	1791	Jury Trial

---

[17] *Amendment Summary: 27 Updates to the U.S. Constitution.* (n.d.-b). https://www.u-s-history.com/pages/h926.html

8th	1791	Protections against Excessive Bail, Cruel and Unusual Punishment
9th	1791	Non-Enumerated Rights
10th	1791	Rights Reserved to States
11th	1795	Suits Against a State
12th	1804	Election of President and Vice-President
13th	1865	Abolition of Slavery and Involuntary Servitude
14th	1868	Protects rights against state infringements, defines citizenship, prohibits states from interfering with privileges and immunities, requires due process and equal protection, punishes states for denying vote, and disqualifies Confederate officials and debts
15th	1870	Voting Rights
16th	1913	Federal Income Tax
17th	1913	Popular Election of Senators
18th	1919	Prohibition
19th	1920	Women's Right to Vote
20th	1933	Commencement of Presidential Term and Succession
21st	1933	Repeal of 18th Amendment (Prohibition)
22nd	1951	Two-Term Limitation on President
23rd	1961	District of Columbia Presidential Vote
24th	1964	Abolition of Poll Tax Requirement in Federal Elections

25th	1967	Presidential Vacancy, Disability, and Inability
26th	1971	Right to Vote at Age 18
27th	1992	Congressional Compensation

Perhaps, it's time for a major overhaul of this document – starting with term limits, a maximum of 8 years for both the House and Senate, which means four two-year terms for a House member and two four- year terms for the Senate. Age limits, the maximum age to run for President, Vice President, House of Representative, and Senate will be capped at age 72. When the constitution was created, members of Congress were meant to be exclusively white men.

As of today, white men represent 66% of the House and 64% of the Senate. There are many qualified and educated individuals of varied backgrounds and ethnicities in this diverse nation who would serve the people well. However, the current system allows members to spend their entire adult life in Congress; being in office that long causes members to lose focus on why they were elected. This allows them to cozy up with big business/corporate Wall Street donors through lobbyist and political action committees (PACs) and manipulate major loopholes in the federal campaign financing & spending law. This makes it almost impossible for a qualified up-and-coming candidate to compete and win a campaign because of the like of money to compete fairly. It is not about the best candidate to serve the people; it is about the amount the money they receive from big business and corporate Wall Street donors.

I highly encourage everyone to read the U.S. Constitution. It is not a long document and does not require you to be a constitutional scholar to understand or interpret. It is "The Supreme Law of the Land," a must-read document for every U.S. citizen. Also, I highly encourage everyone to read Judge Harlan's dissent papers for both cases, "Civil Rights case of 1883" and "Plessy v. Ferguson."

Chapter 2

The Compromised Psyche of the American Missionary Association & Northern Philanthropists and the Black Educational Experience

It would be appropriate to start the chapter with an excerpt from the book "*The Experience of Thomas H. Jones, "Who Was a Slave" for Forty-Three Years.*" In the book, Thomas H. Jones describes an encounter with his master while attempting to learn how to read. Many enslaved Black Americans were self-determined to learn to read and write under the extremely brutal conditions before emancipation which banned them from obtaining any form of knowledge. Below is the excerpt from the book that best defines the state of affairs of those times and how Black Americans were treated by their masters.

"I was at the store early one morning, and, thinking I was safe from all danger for a few minutes, had seated myself in the back store, on one of the barrels, to study in my precious spelling-book. While I was absorbed in this happy enterprise, my master came in, much earlier than usual, and I did not hear him. He came directly into the back store. I saw his shadow on the wall, just in time to throw my book over in among the barrels before he could see what it was, although he saw that I had thrown something quickly away. His suspicion was aroused. He said that I had been stealing something out of the store, and fiercely ordered me to get what I threw away just as he was coming in at the door. Without a moment's hesitation, I determined to save my precious book and my future opportunities to learn from it. I knew if my book was discovered that all was lost, and I felt prepared

for any hazard or suffering rather than give up my book and my hopes for improvement. So, I replied at once to his questions, that I had not thrown anything away; that I had not stolen anything from the store; that I did not have anything in my hands that I could throw away when he came in. My master declared in a high passion, that I was lying, and ordered me to begin and roll away the barrels. This I did; but managed to keep the book slipping along so that he could not see it, as he stood in the door-way. He charged me again with stealing and throwing something away, and I again denied the charge. In a great rage, he got down his long, heavy cow-hide, and ordered me to strip off my jacket and shirt, saying, with an oath, "I will make you tell me what it was you had when I came."

I stripped myself, and came forward, according to his directions, at the same time denying his charge with great earnestness of tone, look, and manner. He cut me on my naked back, perhaps thirty times, with great severity, making the blood flow freely. He then stopped and asked me what I had thrown away as he came in. I answered again that I had thrown nothing away. He swore terribly; said he was certain I was lying and declared he would kill me if I did not tell him the truth. He whipped me the second time with greater severity, and at greater length than before. He then repeated his question, and I answered again as before. I was determined to die if I could possibly bear the pain, rather than give up my dear book. He whipped me the third time, with the same result as before, and then seizing hold of my shoulders, turned me round as though he would inflict on my quivering flesh still another scourging, but he saw the deep gashes he had already made, and the blood already flowing under his cruel infliction; and his stern purpose failed him. He said, "Why, Tom, I

26

didn't think I had cut you so bad," and saying that he stopped, and told me to put on my shirt again.

I did as he bade me, although my coarse shirt touching my raw back put me in cruel pain. He then went out, and I got my book and hid it safely away before he came in again. When I went to the house, my wounds had dried, and I was in an agony of pain. My mistress told the servant girl, Rachel, to help me off with my shirt, and to wash my wounds for me, and put on to them some sweet oil. The shirt was dried to my back so that it could not be got off without tearing off some of the skin with it. The pain, upon doing this, was greater even than I had endured from my cruel whipping.

After Rachel had got my shirt off, my mistress asked me what I had done for which my master had whipped me so severely. I told her he had accused me of stealing when I had not, and then had whipped me to make me own it."[18]

There were many stories like this that were never told. This one instance from the book illustrates a clear picture of Black American slaves before emancipation. Apart from banning them from learning to read and write, they were also subjected to violence at the hands of their masters. This defines the whole power dynamic practiced at that time, dominating generations of Black Americans.

After emancipation, the former enslaved Black Americans were freed into a market economy with no money, land, or basic resources, and because of this, they faced huge challenges in striving to sustain

---

[18]Written by a Friend (1857), *The Experience of Thomas H. Jones, "Who Was a Slave" for Forty-Three Years.* Worcester: Printed by Henry J. Howland, No. 245 Main Street.

themselves economically. Despite the social and economic hardships, their desire to learn to read/write and be educated was of the utmost importance to a people who had mostly been denied this basic human right throughout their entire lives.

During Reconstruction (1863 – 1877), many Black American communities were self-determined and set up schools for themselves and their children. However, with limited resources, many welcomed the support from the northern reformers for assistance, such as the Freedmen's Bureau, the American Missionary Association (AMA), and other northern philanthropist organizations set up to help Black Americans in gaining an education.

The Freedmen's Bureau was established in 1865 by the federal government, responsible for providing relief to the newly freed Black Americans with shelter, food, medical aid, clothing, land, and reuniting family members who had been separated during enslavement. However, President Andrew Johnson was one of the strongest adversaries of the Bureau. In 1866 he vetoed the legislation to extend the powers of the Freedmen's Bureau and its tenure. He also pardoned former Confederates, followed by restoring their land, which signified to white Southerners that they could reclaim racial and social dominance in the Southern States. In 1872, the Freedmen Bureau was abolished by Congress.

The American Missionary Association (AMA) consisted of Christian congregations – Methodist, Presbyterian, American Baptist, and other sects from the north. Their primary purpose was to spread Christian values and to train former enslaved Black Americans to be preachers and teachers. In theory, both objectives were decent endeavors, and possibly, their intentions were well-meaning, but most of these northern Christians were of the mindset that the formerly enslaved Black Americans needed character training to conform to the social order of white supremacy. This is to say all those efforts to teach the former enslaved Black Americans the scriptures were purely based on the idea of them being uncivilized and needing to be taught the ways of the dominant white culture.

The overwhelming emphasis on creating preachers was to have them return to the Black American communities and indoctrinate the masses to keep them submissive. The AMA viewed themselves as the white saviors, with noble intentions and the belief that they knew what was best for the formerly enslaved Black Americans. With all their religious/Christian beliefs, they still perceived human beings who looked different than themselves as heathens, intellectually inferior, and less-than human. Even though most of the AMA members were educated and devoted Christians, they believed in the notion that Black Americans were inferior to them. These thoughts were deeply ingrained in the psyche of northern and Southern whites by the country's social structure, which was shaped by white supremacy.

The AMA and the Bureau collaborated closely to establish hundreds of schools/private colleges and provided teachers for the formerly enslaved Black Americans in the Southern States. After the Bureau's abolishment, several men continued their work at the private Black colleges that were established under the Bureau and the American Missionary Association. Notably, General Oliver O. Howard, known as the "Christian General" in the union army, was co-founder of Howard Normal and Theological Institute for the Education of Preachers and Teachers, a theological seminary to train

Black American ministers. The name was later changed to what we know today as Howard University. General Howard served as president of these private colleges from 1867 - 1873. General Samuel C. Armstrong, the co-founder of Hampton Institute, known today as Hampton University, served as the president from 1868 – 1893. General Armstrong was the mastermind behind the industrial training curriculum and laid the blueprint for why it should be implemented in the schools/colleges established for the former enslaved Black Americans.

On the surface, their commitment to the cause of Black American education was honorable. However, their main objective was reuniting the northern and Southern States so that the country would be economically viable and socially stable and ensure that the former enslaved Black Americans maintained a bottom caste status in order to maintain the social order of white supremacy.

In 1876 to settle the dispute regarding the U.S. Presidential election between Rutherford B. Hayes and Samuel J. Tilden, Democrats and Republicans, members of Congress compromised on a deal to have Rutherford B. Hayes elected president of the United States in 1877. In return, Rutherford B. Hayes removed the federal troops from the Southern States, with the agenda that Democrat control would prevail over the region. Today this is known as the compromise of 1877.

After the civil war, federal troops were sent to the Southern States to ensure the new laws were enforced and to avert any uprising from the Southern white planter's class or Southern white supremacists. When Rutherford B. Hayes ordered the removal of the troops, the

Reconstruction Era effectively ended, which ushered in retaliation by the Southern white supremacist, which consisted of bitterly hostile, unrelenting terrorization, violence, destruction (burning down of many black schools that were built across the south), and murder. The federal government relinquished control/oversight and turned a blind eye to the Southern State's affairs, which led to a blatant disregard for the fourteenth and fifteenth amendments. The Southern white supremacists/legislatures ignored the U.S. Constitution (the supreme law of the land) and enacted laws separating human beings in public spaces by race, and thus the Jim Crow laws ensued.

Despite the abolishment of the Bureau, and the Reconstruction Era ending, the American Missionary Association continued to actively provide teachers and co-found schools/colleges throughout the Southern States. However, their mission now depended heavily on the money from the northern white philanthropists to sustain their objectives. The powerful northern white philanthropists seized the opportunity with the likes of the Phelps Stokes Fund, Peabody Education Fund, Slater Fund for the Education of Freedmen, and the General Education Board (GEB). These northern white philanthropists in power governed the results of the initiative and benefited highly from these initiatives as well. These powerful northern white philanthropists joined in the educational caravan, supporting the AMA mission by funding the schools/private colleges established for the formerly enslaved Black Americans in the Southern States. Putting them in absolute control of leadership positions to choose the curriculum and educational goals for the schools/colleges. The northern white philanthropists became the brain trust behind the education for the former enslaved Black Americans in the Southern States.

The American Missionary Association, coupled with these powerful northern white philanthropists, made considerable investments in establishing schools and private Black colleges, which was a mere fraction compared to the substantial sum of money the founders of these northern white philanthropist organizations made directly or indirectly from chattel slavery or the slave trade which played a major role in them accumulating their wealth.

Northern White Philanthropists' Influence and Control in Black Education

The Peabody Education Fund, the Slater Fund, the General Education Board (GEB), and the Phelps-Stokes Fund were organizations established in the 19th and early 20th centuries to support the initiative of educating former enslaved Black Americans in the Southern United States. However, the major drawback of all these organizations was that the individuals influencing and controlling decision-making were all dedicated to keeping the former enslaved Black Americans at the bottom of society. Their primary goal was to develop and guarantee that the southern agricultural economic system remained intact by promoting industrial training and Christian education to the formerly enslaved Black Americans. It ensured continuous access to cheap labor and maintained the southern racial hierarchy of white supremacy.

The **Peabody Education Fund** was established in 1867 by George Peabody, a philanthropist and financier, after the Civil War.

The general agent for the fund was Jabez Lamar Monroe (J.L.M.) Curry from 1881–1903. The fund was established to promote industrial and moral training for former enslaved Black Americans in the Southern United States.

John Fox Slater established the **Slater Fund** in 1882. He was a philanthropist who believed that education and Christianity were the keys to improving the lives of Black Americans. Rutherford B. Hayes chaired its governing board, and its general agents were Atticus Green Haygood, J.L.M. Curry, Wallace Buttrick, and James H. Dillard. The fund supported establishing schools that provided domestic science and industrial arts training, particularly emphasizing attaining those disciplines for Black American women, with a significant focus on teaching skills such as cooking, sewing, and home economics.

The **Phelps Stokes Fund** was established in 1911 by Caroline Phelps Stokes, a philanthropist and member of the Phelps Stokes family. In 1912, Thomas Jesse Jones was appointed the educational director of the fund. He was also an associate chaplain and instructor at Hampton Institute. This fund also focuses on providing financial assistance to schools and institutions committed to industrial training and Christian education.

The **General Education Board (GEB)** was established in 1902 by John D. Rockefeller. William H. Baldwin Jr. became the fund's first president and served as a trustee at Tuskegee Institute. J.L.M. Curry was a member of the board of directors. The fund was established to promote education throughout the United States, but its primary focus was the education of Black Americans in the Southern States. It was also the only entity that outpaced all the other initiatives in terms of size, scope, and longevity, which were introduced to educate Black Americans. Even though the initiative was introduced in an attempt to reduce racial segregation, it did not specifically operate on such objectives; thus, the results obtained from the initiative did not show racial equity of any form.

The GEB also launched an agriculture development program to help improve the economic base for public schools across the rural South, emphasizing the need for Blacks to learn farming and other labor skills.

The South still enforced segregation, so the GEB set up different public schools for Black Americans and white students. The Black American schools were named "Country Training Schools" and promoted egregious industrial/vocational training and domestic science curriculums, while the white schools promoted academic subjects. All these efforts were made to appease the social order of the Southern States.

The compromising psyche of the American Missionary Association and the powerful northern white philanthropists meant cooperating with the Southern States' social order of white supremacy to maintain segregation and promote Christian and industrial training for Black Americans. They established a policy of inequity in allocating funds and controlled the institutions by keeping them out of Black Americans' reach by all means. All the positions of power were held by white individuals, which further ensured that the policies and educational system were sustained in a way to deceive Black Americans about the complexities of Christianity, so there were no means for them to challenge their authority collectively.

While some private colleges offered liberal arts curriculums, most of the money from the northern philanthropic organizations was channeled into the private colleges and the "country training schools", which offered industrial education and moral/practical training curriculums. These curriculums focused on introducing students to industrial training, Christian morality, housekeeping, personal hygiene, gardening, and the southern racial etiquette of not appearing uppity or threatening the social order of white supremacy. The private liberal arts colleges were poorly funded, and many were forced to implement industrial curriculums in order to receive funding from the wealthy northern white philanthropists' organizations. They were determined to treat the former enslaved Black Americans practically as objects they could control.

All things considered; it can be established that all these organizations were presented as an initiative to support Black Americans' education. In reality, the administrators had an ulterior motive of maintaining the social order of white supremacy. Even though these organizations had several members, the four most prominent members played a significant role in developing and succeeding these programs. Those members were: Wallace Buttrick, William H. Baldwin Jr., J.L.M. Curry, and Thomas Jesse Jones. I have quoted below each of the members' views regarding the matter of education for Black Americans, which evidently portray their emphasis on only providing them industrial training instead of any real form of education that they desperately needed. Reading these quotes, you would be better able to deduce their real intentions behind launching these organizations that showcased upfront that they were helping the former slaves.

William Henry Baldwin, who was appointed as the first president of the GEB and served as a trustee of the Tuskegee Institute, believed Black Americans were only suited for the bottom caste of society. He made several such remarks about Black American citizens, one of which is quoted below:

"I believe in helping the negro to help himself, and to my mind, the best way to do this is to equip him with intelligent industrial training. The accumulation of a mess of knowledge that cannot be used is a waste of time. Except in the rarest of instances, I am bitterly opposed to the so-called higher education for negroes. I believe in training them in practical ways."[19]

L. M. Curry, who proved himself prominent in several different foundations, is shown to have written:

"The white people are to be the leaders, to have the initiative, to have the directive control in all matters pertaining to civilization and the highest interests of our beloved land. History demonstrates that the Caucasian will rule. He ought to rule. This white supremacy does not mean hostility to the Negro, but friendship for him."[20]

Thomas Jesse Jones advocated for promoting the Hampton Institute industrial training curriculum for all Black Americans, which infuriated Dr. Carter G. Woodson and W.E.B. Du Bois, considering

---

[19]Walsh, Barbara. H. (1974). *The Negro and His Education: Persuasive Strategies of Selected Speeches at the Conference for Education in the South, 1898-1914.* LSU Digital Commons. https://digitalcommons.lsu.edu/gradschool_disstheses/2769/

[20]Peeps, J.M. Stephen. "Northern Philanthropy and the Emergence of Black Higher Education---Do --Gooders, Compromisers, or Co-Conspirators?" *The Journal of Negro Education, vol. 50, no. 3, 1981, pp. 251–69. JSTOR, https://doi.org/10.2307/2295156. Accessed 3 Apr. 2021.*

Jones's influence over philanthropic organizations. Du Bois labeled him the "evil genius of the Black race" in 1919. A 1917 study on the Negro education, under the direction of Jones, reported that *"Southern Blacks were essentially rural and required agricultural education, that the economic prosperity of the Black south rested with manual labor, and that northern wealth and political power which was exercised by the whites were needed to continue to shape the south."*[21]

Wallace Buttrick held the belief that the education of Black people should be limited to certain "useful" fields. According to him, Black American schools should *"teach agriculture and related industries"* and support *"such training of the Negro for the life that now is, as shall make of him a producer—a servant—of his day and generation of the highest sense."*[22]

It was not just a single organization that put forward the instructions that reeked of prejudice, but all of them. Under the disguise of northern reformers providing educational funding to the Black American schools/private colleges in the Southern States, they were of the belief that those former slaves could not succeed in more advanced fields of study. Even the teachers assumed Black Americans did not have the innate ability to comprehend and grasp advanced knowledge. This belief was rooted in the racist idea that Black Americans were intellectually inferior to whites.

---

[21]Watkins, William, H. (2001). *The White Architects of Black Education: Ideology and Power in America, 1865-1954.* Teachers College Press, New York.

[22]Goldberg, Barry and Shubinski, Barbara. (2020). *Black Education and Rockefeller Philanthropy from the Jim Crow South to the Civil Rights Era - REsource.* REsource. https://resource.rockarch.org/story/black-education-and-rockefeller-philanthropy-from-the-jim-crow-south-to-the-civil-rights-era/

Moreover, these organizations were established and managed by northern white philanthropists, and the funding allocation was done without proper representation or participation of the Black American community. This lack of representation and participation made reaching a viable solution that best suited Black Americans impossible. They consciously introduced policies and curriculums that were primarily focused on the development of an efficient, stable southern agricultural economy at the cost of restricting Black Americans to a negligible form of education.

All these efforts were influenced by the prejudices held against Black Americans. The majority of white Americans believed that Black Americans could not benefit from higher education and would be better served by learning practical skills that could be used in manual labor and domestic work. This belief was rooted in the racist and discriminatory attitudes that existed in American society at the time, which persist even today.

Reflecting on all the objectives administered through the fund gives us a clear picture of the main objective of the people in power; every step taken in the name of the betterment of Black Americans was shadowed by anti-Blackness.

The "Negro Question" at Mohonk

The Mohonk Conference of 1890 was held at Lake Mohonk in Ulster County, New York. The first of the two conferences held at Lake Mohonk was on the "Negro Question," while the second conference was held later, in 1891. The attendees were leaders from various sectors of American society, including politics, business, education, and religion.

The conference was hosted by Albert K. Smiley, an educator, and owner of the Mohonk property. The group believed that the "Negro Question" was a notable problem that required attention and that this conference was an opportunity for leaders from various sectors of American society to come together to exchange views on solutions for improving the situation of the Black American population in the Southern States.

Rutherford B. Hayes, the ex-president of the United States, chaired this first conference, the same man who compromised with the Southern Democrats and ordered the removal of the federal troops from the Southern States, which ended the Reconstruction Era. I cannot make this stuff up; this is accurate history which is never told in history textbooks.

During the conference, participants discussed a wide range of topics related to Black Americans, including education, labor, politics, and civil rights. Many of the participants believed that the key to solving the "Negro Question" was through Christianization and industrial training, as they believed that this would help to improve the economic status of Black Americans and assimilate them into mainstream White American society.

However, many of the conference's discussions and recommendations were based on the idea of "civilizing and character building," which was a colonialist perspective. This perspective suggested that it was the duty of the White people to train and uplift the Black American population in order to make them more like the supposedly "civilized" White society according to the standards set by them.

It's important to note that the Mohonk conferences did not reflect the perspectives of the Black American community, nor did they consider the systemic issues of racism and discrimination at the core of the "Negro Question" perpetuated by the white dominant American culture. This is because the conferences were organized and controlled by white individuals who had little interest in hearing the perspectives or concerns of Black Americans.

This lack of representation of Black American perspectives in the conference led to a lack of understanding of the unique challenges and issues faced by Black Americans daily. This also resulted in solutions and recommendations based on stereotypes and misconceptions rather than on an accurate understanding of the situation and needs of the Black American community.

The participants were more interested in providing solutions to the "Negro Question" based on their own perceptions of what was best for the Black American community than listening to their needs and concerns.

Overall, the absence of Black Americans at the Mohonk conferences was a major limitation, and it hindered the ability of the conference to produce meaningful solutions to the challenges faced by Black Americans. It also highlighted the broader issue of the exclusion of Black Americans from mainstream American society and the lack of interest among white Americans to truly understand

and address the issues faced by the Black American community. The bottom line is that the conferences did not bring significant changes to the lives of Black Americans.

Here are a few excerpts from the speeches given at this conference by Christian leaders on what was best for the former enslaved Black Americans:

Samuel C. Armstrong was the first president of Hampton University from 1868–1893 and the architect behind the industrial training curriculum for former enslaved Black Americans.

"Under the auspices of the American Missionary Association, I was asked to take charge of the work in Hampton; and we worked the thing out, acting on principles which we have carried out ever since. The great trouble with the Negro was not ignorance: it was the deficiency of character. You can feed and clothe the Negro, build his home, and give him knowledge; but that does not necessarily build up character. That has got to be worked out. The conditions of character and manhood and citizenship for all people are simple and clear. Our salvation is nearer to us than we suppose. The progress and uplifting of the Negro are attainable more readily than we think. On these ideas, we organized our school and industrial system, which has been written up by Miss Alice Bacon in the last Southern Workman."[23]

Rev. Dr. A. F. Beard, Corresponding Secretary of the American Missionary Association, New York.

---

[23]Barrows, Isabel, C. (1890). *First Mohonk Conference On The Negro Question: Held At Lake Mohonk, Ulster County, New York, June 4, 5, 6, 1890.* George H. Ellis, Printer. pp. 7-137.

"This appears to be a kind of experience meeting. It is well that this industrial feature of saving the people comes first upon our program. It came in this order when our first parents were commanded to attend to agricultural work. I quite agree with General Armstrong in the assertion that the thing to be sought for in elevating a people is character. First and last, and all the time, what is needed is character. If we can get right character, all other issues will be right. If we can settle the question of character, the question of race is settled".[24]

"The missionary idea is the emphatic idea of the schools sustained by us. We seek, first of all, to make Christians; and we connect with our Christian schools' industrial schools, because they are adjuncts in the building of character. I quite agree, also, with Dr. Allen in the necessity of accentuating the education for girls. We must save the girls for the homes, and for generations to come. We have, therefore, introduced industrial accompaniments in all of our schools for girls. I am sure that General Armstrong is not out of the way in the emphasis which he places upon industry as a foundation for character, for there are certain lacks in the negro which perhaps can be met only by this industrial training".[25]

"Again, the untrained Negro lacks accuracy. 'Almost' and 'altogether' mean the same thing to the Negro. His 'pretty near' is

---

[24]Barrows, Isabel, C. (1890). *First Mohonk Conference On The Negro Question: Held At Lake Mohonk, Ulster County, New York, June 4, 5, 6, 1890*. George H. Ellis, Printer. pp. 7-137.

[25]Barrows, Isabel, C. (1890). *First Mohonk Conference On The Negro Question: Held At Lake Mohonk, Ulster County, New York, June 4, 5, 6, 1890*. George H. Ellis, Printer. pp. 7-137.

the same as absolute right. 'It will do' is well enough for him. He is inconsiderate in work. Industrial education helps to overcome this."[26]

Rev. R. H. Allen, D.D., Corresponding Secretary of the Board of Missions for the Freedmen of the Presbyterian Church.

"If you ever save the Negroes, you must save the girls and women. You will not elevate any race until wives and mothers can teach the gospel in their families. You must save the daughters of the freedmen. They are to be the wives and mothers and homemakers of the future. At Concord you will see two hundred and thirty-four girls in a seminary, with all the appliances for education and the industrial arts. They do the whole work of the school, - all the washing, ironing, cooking, scrubbing, and dressmaking."[27]

The main point to consider is that each of these men were followers of the Christian faith, claiming to have moral standards and beliefs while, at the same time, they were acting in their own personal interests. The lone act of the conference, which did not include any single Black American person, was, in fact, an example of the moral standards and character they claimed to act upon.

The indoctrination of Christianity was the means through which white supremacy prevailed. In the book "Narrative of the Life of Frederick Douglass," which was one of the three autobiographies he wrote during his lifetime, he recounts what happened to him – or what had not happened to him – after his master, Thomas Auld, became a

---

[26]Barrows, Isabel, C. (1890). *First Mohonk Conference On The Negro Question: Held At Lake Mohonk, Ulster County, New York, June 4, 5, 6, 1890*. George H. Ellis, Printer. pp. 7-137.

[27]Barrows, Isabel, C. (1890). *First Mohonk Conference On The Negro Question: Held At Lake Mohonk, Ulster County, New York, June 4, 5, 6, 1890*. George H. Ellis, Printer. pp. 7-137.

Christian believer. While Douglass was hoping that Auld's conversion would make him kind and humane, he writes, *"If it had any effect on his character, it made him more cruel and hateful in all his ways."*[28]

Auld would participate day and night in revivals, praying the entire day. He would open his home to preachers yet would inflict as much pain and suffering upon slaves as he could muster. Douglass also writes, *"I have seen him tie up a lame young woman, and whip her with a heavy cowskin upon her naked shoulders, causing the warm red blood to drip; and, in justification of the bloody deed, he would quote this passage of Scripture— "He that knoweth his master's will, and doeth it not, shall be beaten with many stripes."*[29]

For this reason, for all that he had seen, Douglass remains scornful of Christianity in all his memoirs. He argued that Christianity was a 'slaveholding religion of this land' – nothing but 'the boldest of all frauds.' The slave masters used the excerpts from the Bible to justify most of the acts of violence that were performed on the slaves.

Spirituality should be personal, and when the African slaves were brought to this country, I am sure they all had their own religious or spiritual beliefs. The First Amendment to the U.S. Constitution (the supreme law of the land) says an individual has the right to exercise their chosen faith or choose not to follow any religion. Religion should never be used as a means to abuse and

---

[28]Douglass, Frederick. (1845). *"Narrative of the Life of Frederick Douglass: An American Slave, Written by Himself." The Anti-Slavery Office.*

[29]Douglass, Frederick. (1845). *"Narrative of the Life of Frederick Douglass: An American Slave, Written by Himself." The Anti-Slavery Office.*

control people for economic gains and industrial exploitation in the personal interests of those in power. Deliberately indoctrinating people into an ideology that the indoctrinators did not conform to was pure hypocrisy and an abuse of power

However, according to the Pew Research Center (2022), a nonpartisan fact tank that informs the public about issues, attitudes, and trends shaping the world, the indoctrination apparently worked and has been passed down from generation to generation in the Black community. Nevertheless, as a collective, the majority of Black communities are still marginalized in this country today.

Do the numbers in the survey below indicate its effectiveness?

- Belief in God; absolutely - by race/ethnicity

    o Black 83%

    o White 61%

    o Asian 44%

    o Latino 59%

    o Other 66%

- Importance of religion in one's life; very important – by race/ethnicity

    o Black 75%

    o White 49%

- Asian 36%

- Latino 59%

- Other 54%

- Attendance at religious service; very important – by race/ethnicity

    - Black 47%

    - White 34%

    - Asian 20%

    - Latino 39%

    - Other 34%

Pew Research Center Religious Landscape Study survey data above shows the following in the United States.:[30]

This is not the only form of hypocrisy I would like to bring to your attention. These charitable organizations controlled every aspect of the private historically Black colleges/universities (HBCUs), from implementing inferior training curriculums, poor funding, and appointing White presidents to oversee the institution to naming the segregated private colleges/universities after themselves. Their mentality was equivalent to that of the former slave owners when

[30] *Religion in America: U.S. Religious Data, Demographics and Statistics | Pew Research Center.* (2022). Pew Research Center's Religion & Public Life Project. https://www.pewresearch.org/religion/religious-landscape-study/racial-and-ethnic-composition/

he/she purchased a person; they established his/her duties, gave the person his/her surname, and never compensated him/her for their labor. This is another example of how the social structure of white supremacy shaped their psyche.

They were reluctant to trust a Black American with the control of most of these institutions until around the mid-twentieth century. For example, Fisk University's first Black president was not appointed until 1946, Hampton University in 1949, Spelman College in 1953, Tougaloo College in 1964, Stillman College in 1966, Xavier University in New Orleans – the only HBCU established by the Catholic Church, appointed its first Black president in 1968. Followed by Paine College, appointing its first Black president in 1971. Many cynics have stated that the institutions hired their first Black presidents because they wanted a convenient scapegoat if the institutions were to fail.[31]

The list below contains most of the private HBCUs that are named after a white person associated with the above-mentioned Freedmen Bureau/AMA/philanthropist organizations:

- Howard University – founded in 1866 by the American Missionary Association as the Howard Normal and Theological Institution for training Preachers, and 1867 changed its name to Howard University after Union General Oliver O. Howard, known as the "Christian General" a white

---

[31] The Tradition of White Presidents at Black Colleges." *The Journal of Blacks in Higher Education*, No. 16, 1997, pp. 93–99. *JSTOR*, https://doi.org/10.2307/2962918. Accessed 20 Dec. 2021.

union army General, in charge of the Freedmen Bureau. Died on October 26, 1909.

- Fisk University – founded in 1866 by the American Missionary Association as the Fisk School, and in 1867 changed its name to Fisk University after Clinton B. Fisk, a white man union army Brigadier General and member of the Tennessee Freedmen Bureau. Died on July 9, 1890.

- Morehouse College – founded in 1867 by the American Missionary Association as the Augusta Institute, changed its name in 1879 to Atlanta Baptist Seminary, in 1897 changed its name to Atlanta Baptist College, and in 1913 it was renamed to Morehouse College after Henry L. Morehouse, a white Baptist minister, and member of the American Baptist Home Mission Society. Died on May 5, 1917.

- Atlanta Clark University – founded in 1869 by the American Missionary Association as Clark College, changed its name in 1877 to Clark University, after Bishop Davis W. Clark, a white Bishop of the Methodist Episcopal Church, and the first president of the Freedmen's Aid Society. Died on May 23, 1871. In 1988 it was renamed Clark Atlanta University.

- Rust College – founded in 1866 by the Freedmen's Aid Society, as Rust College for adults and children, for instruction in elementary subjects. Changed its name in 1870 to Shaw University, and in 1892 was renamed back to Rust College after Richard S. Rust, a white American Methodist preacher, secretary of the Freedmen's Bureau, and founder of the Freedmen's Aid Society. Died on December 22, 1906.

- Spelman College - Founded in 1881 by Sophia B. Packard and Harriet E. Giles as Atlanta Baptist Female Seminary. In 1882,

Packard and Giles introduced the female seminary to John D. Rockefeller, who donated $250 to the school. In 1884, the name was changed to Spelman Seminary after Laura Spelman Rockefeller, the wife of John D. Rockefeller. In 1924, the name was changed to Spelman College.

- Dillard University – founded in 1930 by John H. Dillard J. H. Dillard, an educator, general agent for the Slater Fund, and the son of slaveholders. Dillard University was established with the merger of New Orleans University and Straight College. Both were founded with support from the American Missionary Association.

I know some will say that they invested their resources and had the right to name the institution whatever they desired. However, my counter-argument is that they named the university after themselves because they considered themselves superior and suffered from an inflated psyche and self-aggrandizement, which is an endemic found among many White people in this country. I would speculate that the naming of these institutions had very little input from the Black Americans they were supposedly helping.

Below is the lone public school not affiliated with the above-mentioned charitable organizations, but also named after a white person.

- Alcorn State University – The first federal land-grant Historically Black College/University, not affiliated with the American Missionary Association or philanthropist money. Founded in 1871, Alcorn University changed its name in 1878 to Alcorn Agricultural & Mechanical College, and in 1974 it was renamed Alcorn State University. The institution was named after James L. Alcorn, a slave owner, Confederate brigadier general during the Civil War, U.S. Senator during the Reconstruction Era, and Governor of Mississippi in 1871, when federal land-grant funds were allocated to the state to establish a segregated public college for Black Americans. Alcorn was so arrogant he named the college in his own honor. He was known as a racist, and his opposition to Mississippi civil rights legislation, along with his refusal to employ local black officers where a white person could be found, were some of the highlights of his tenure.

The key takeaway here is that they are historical "BLACK" colleges/universities, and as you can see above, the naming went through several iterations, so why not name the institution after the first Black graduate or the first Black student? Or, in the case of Alcorn State University, why not after the first Black president of the institution – Hiram R. Revels, "Hiram State University" or "Revels State University"? As I have stated above, their intentions may have been honorable. However, in the grand scheme of things, their actions were focused on appeasing white Southerners and managing the racial conflicts in the Southern States to safeguard the post-civil war new social, political, and industrial order of white supremacy.

I am not criticizing or disparaging these great institutions! I am sharing the true history and the inflated psyche/arrogance of these Christian white men, which is not commonly discussed. My attempt in this whole analysis is just to show the prevailing hypocrisy/hidden agenda in the advancement of these so-called institutions to help Black Americans. The institutions were poorly funded then, if they did not comply with the northern white philanthropists', and can still be considered poorly funded to this day.

In closing this chapter, I would like to include an instance I recently encountered. I was watching the 2022 college national championship football game between the University of Alabama and the University of Georgia, both public land-grant universities. I noticed that perhaps over 90 percent of the players/gladiators on the field were descendants of former enslaved Black Americans, and when the camera person focused the camera on the fans in the stadium, I noticed over 90 percent of the fans were white. Both institutions were adamant about not allowing the ancestors of these players to be admitted to either of these schools, and the first athletic scholarship offered to a Black American did not occur until 1967.

The University of Alabama did not admit its first Black student until 1956. According to the Office of Institutional Research and Assessment, today, the enrollment breakdown is 74.37% White, 11.16% Black, 5.32% Hispanic/Latino, 1.54% Asian, and 0.36% American Indian/Alaska Native[32].

The University of Georgia did not admit its first Black student until 1961 after the students won a legal battle to gain admission.

Data USA shared a chart defining the number of students that were enrolled at the University of Georgia. Today the enrollment

---

[32] The University of Alabama. (n.d.). Students by Race/Ethnicity. Retrieved March 2, 2023, from oira.ua.edu website: https://oira.ua.edu/factbook/reports/student-enrollment/fall-term/students-by-race-ethnicity/

breakdown is 66.7% White, 8.22% Asian, 5.72% Black, 4.06% Hispanic/Latino, and 0.115% American Indian/Alaska Native[33].

Some would say this is progress! However, both universities' Black enrollments are below the 13.6% Black population in the country. What would the Black student enrollment percentage look like if all the Black athletes woke up tomorrow and decided to enroll at Historically Black Colleges and Universities?

---

[33] University of Georgia. (n.d.). University of Georgia | Data USA. Retrieved from datausa.io website: https://datausa.io/profile/university/university-of-georgia

Chapter 3
Hollywood Anti-Black Propaganda and The Effect on The Psyche

The history of iniquities in Hollywood goes as far back as the first blockbuster movie of its time. As I briefly mentioned in chapter one, President Woodrow Wilson contributed to the sweeping endorsement of the Hollywood motion picture industry, producing films depicting negative and racial stereotypes of Black Americans during his tenure. He viewed the film 'The Birth of a Nation' at a special White House screening and reportedly stated, "*It's like writing history with lightning. My only regret is that it is all so terribly true,*"[34] effusively supporting one of the most racist movies in American history.

However, not only was the film viewed at the White House, but the next night the film was shown to a large audience at the National Press Club, including Chief Justice Edward Douglas White, who served on the U.S. Supreme Court for 27 years and as Chief Justice from 1910–1921. Also present were 38 senators and 50 members of the House of Representatives, along with several other members of the Supreme Court at that time. This was an across-the-board endorsement from all three branches of government, giving Hollywood the green light to release the film to the general public.

"Birth of a Nation" went on to become the first Hollywood blockbuster and the highest-grossing film of that time; it was a huge

---

[34]Benbow, Mark E. "Birth of a Quotation: Woodrow Wilson and 'Like Writing History with Lightning.'" *The Journal of the Gilded Age and Progressive Era*, vol. 9, no. 4, 2010, pp. 509–33. *JSTOR*, http://www.jstor.org/stable/20799409.

success. White Americans were fascinated by watching Black Americans in such a negative light; it influenced American culture and helped mold public opinion. Consequently, Hollywood discovered the blueprint for further shaping the psyche of the American people by producing anti-Black unflattering stereotypes of Black Americans in films and television for mass consumption. It was part of the popular culture in the U.S. media at the turn of the twentieth century. The negative stereotypical views perpetuated about Black Americans were popular among whites, making way for the Hollywood media conglomerate to consciously capitalize on the opportunity with no regard for how it influenced society's psyche.

In this chapter, I will concisely talk about the stereotypical roles created for Black American actors/actresses by the Hollywood film/television industry and highlight several films/TV shows that had a significant impact on further shaping the psyche of the American people.

First, I think we can agree that the power of the Hollywood film/television industry plays a major role in influencing individuals' attitudes, beliefs, and behavior and is the most powerful visual medium for doing this outside of the family, especially throughout the 20th century and continues to this day.

Stereotypical Roles:

Since its inception in the Hollywood film and television industry, Black American characters have been overwhelmingly portrayed in an unfavorable, negative light. In the early to mid-20th century, it was common to see the following character portrayed:

Black American Males

The Tom character was portrayed as obedient, happy, faithful, loyal, servile, asexual, and more than anything, he wanted to please the white man.

The Coon character was portrayed as lazy, buffoonish, frightened, idle, inarticulate, and unhappy. Along with that, he was portrayed as a character incapable of changing his destiny because of his lack of ambition.

The Sambo character was portrayed as happy, loyal, pleased with being a servant or slave, having the mind of a child who could not live on his own, and defending his plight.

The Buck character was portrayed as animalistic, aggressive, violent, destructive, and a predator toward white women who deserved punishment or death.

Black American Females

The Mammy character was portrayed as a sassy, loyal servant, a happy, obese, argumentative, rough woman, and above all, one who loved her white family.

The Jezebel character was portrayed as seductive, lustful, enticing, tempting, and promiscuous. This character was usually played by a fair-complexioned Black female with European features.

The Sapphire character was portrayed as angry, rude, stubborn, abusive, unhappy, bitter, mean-spirited, and known as the Angry Black Woman.

The Welfare Queen character was portrayed as single, hypersexual, with several children, and just mooches off the system.

However, white male actors are overwhelmingly portrayed as brave, handsome, virile, saviors, and godlike. Additionally, white female actresses are overwhelmingly portrayed as pristine, reserved, self-controlled, goddess-like, and as the symbol and standard of American beauty.

All of this was done to reaffirm the dominant white cultural beliefs and to further shape the psyche of the whole American society, including white and Black American citizens, rather than the true experiences and culture of Black Americans. These negative, anti-Black characters were disproportionately shown, with very little positive portrayal of Black Americans in film or television at that time.

Below are examples of several films and television shows across the decades that had high grossing ratings and portrayed the negative stereotypes described above.

The film *Birth of a Nation* (1915) glorified the Ku Klux Klan (KKK) as the nation's white savior and used white actors in blackface to portray the Black American Buck character. Destructive, savage, and aggressively lusting after white women. The movie implied the eradication of Black American men through violence, as Black Americans were an active danger to society and 'American' values. As I mentioned above, the film was a Hollywood blockbuster and the highest-grossing film of that time.

Following the movie's debut, there was a resurgence of the KKK, and racial violence splurged in the United States against Black Americans, resulting in mass massacres.

In the film *Gone with the Wind* (1939), Hattie McDaniel received an Academy Award for the role of Best Supporting Actress; the irony is that she was portraying and perpetuating a stereotype in her character of a feisty, quick-tempered Mammy who was servile, docile, and non-threatening, serving the sole purpose of keeping the white family satisfied. 'Gone with the Wind' was another Hollywood blockbuster that dethroned 'Birth of a Nation' as the highest-grossing film.

In the 1956 film '*The Ten Commandments*,' all the biblical figures were played by white actors: Charlton Heston as Moses, Yul Bynner as Rameses II, Anne Baxter as Nefretiri, and John Derek as Joshua. This film received nominations for seven Academy Awards and was the highest-grossing film in 1956. It was a blatant example of how Hollywood portrays white actors/actresses in a positive, powerful, and godlike way. The deliberate casting of this film implants the idea into people's psyches that the most significant biblical figures are white and influences them to believe it as well. This film is still being shown today during the Easter/Passover season.

The popular TV show *Tarzan* premiered from 1966 to 1968, narrating the story of a superhuman white man played by Ron Ely. He was the King of the African jungle and could communicate with and defeat the animals with his bare hands, a skill the indigenous Africans could not master. Tarzan was more intelligent and stronger than the indigenous Africans, and, in some episodes, his pet chimpanzee could outsmart the indigenous Africans as well. The narrative was continued in this TV show, portraying indigenous Africans as savages or cannibals, barely evolving above wild animals. This show portrayed a demeaning image of the indigenous people by dehumanizing them. Yet another example of portraying the white man as brave, intelligent, superior, and the savior.

From the mid- to late-20th century, the film industry began producing content about the Black American environment as a representation of Black American culture. Nevertheless, it is crucial to emphasize that many viewers were not and still are not aware of the fact that federal policy and state laws created the Black American environment, and the Hollywood film/television industry was promoting the Black American environment as its culture. The representation of Black Americans in these movies was done by the white people in power, whose prejudices were apparent in every piece of art they created.

Black American men were increasingly portrayed as violent drug dealers, pimps, and gangsters, a modified version of the "Buck character mentioned above." Blaxploitation films were made to intentionally exploit Black American men and women by reinforcing racial prejudice and stereotypes. Movies like *Superfly* (1972), *Black Caesar* (1973), and *Dolemite* (1975), to name a few, became some of the most noted and popular films during the early '70s.

Black women were not spared from the Blaxploitation films; movies like *Coffy* (1973) and *Foxy Brown* (1974) portrayed Black American women as drug addicts, prostitutes, and deviance in nature, the modified version of Sapphire and Jezebel's characters as mentioned above. In both films, the Black American female lead was portrayed as a vengeful vigilante, posing as a prostitute seeking revenge and going on a killing spree to kill a Black male drug dealer in the community. It also addresses the stereotype of the objectification of Black American women. There were certain views that prevailed over the stereotypes and carried one primary plot to reinforce white superiority and negative Black stereotypes. Both films were written, directed, and produced by white men.

In the 1974 film *Claudine*, which was supposedly a love story, the Black American female lead portrayed the "Welfare Queen" character, who is a single mother with an absentee Black American father from a dysfunctional family with six kids, living in a small apartment in New York City, and working as a domestic for a white couple. There were regular inspections by the welfare department to ensure she was not scamming the system by having a man live with her in the apartment. She eventually finds love with the neighborhood garbage collector and lives happily ever after. However, the most intriguing thing about this film was the soundtrack. The good music distracted most of the Black American viewers from seeing the negative stereotypical perception the director, writer, and producer had about Black American families.

As an eleven-year-old kid in 1974, I remember watching this film and thinking it was such a great movie, seeing all the Black actors and the great music. And not understanding the anti-Black stereotype subliminal messages it was conveying.

In the TV show *Sanford and Son's,* which premiered from 1972 to 1977, Esther Anderson played the character 'Aunt Esther.' She portrays the "Sapphire" character as an angry Black American woman with a disdainful relationship with her brother-in-law Fred, played by Redd Foxx. She was boisterous, disrespectful, Bible-carrying, and married to a mild-mannered alcoholic, Woodrow, whom she dominated. In this relationship, the idea of an aggressive Black American woman dominating a weak, morally defective Black American man was also portrayed.

Good Times, a TV show that premiered from 1974 to 1979, was about a Black family living in a public housing project in Chicago, perpetually in poverty. The father, James Evans, is played by John Amos, who could barely provide for his family because of inconsistent employment. Meanwhile, his wife, Florida Evans, was shown as a devoted mother who often prayed to white Jesus for help and was always focused on doing the right thing. Their oldest son, JJ, is portrayed as the "Coon" character, an incompetent buffoon who barely made it through high school and could not fend for himself or his family.

The show made it quite clear that the theme was that no matter how hard the Evans family would pray to white Jesus, they were consistently stuck in a never-ending cycle of perpetual bad luck and poverty. One hundred and thirty-three episodes and no uplift—what were the producers sensationalizing? Wrapped in a disguise of light-hearted humor, they were planting the seed in the psyche of Black Americans that if they are living in poverty, all they can do is pray to white Jesus because they are doomed to a lifelong struggle in a country of abundance.

As I mentioned above, the negative anti-Black characters created by the Hollywood film and television industry in the early 20th century have been modernized to adapt to the current times. The high-grossing films below portrayed some of these modern-day anti-Black characters; the only difference today is that the audience are now worldwide.

In 2001, in the film "Training Day," a Black American police detective, Alonzo, played by Denzel Washington, portrayed the modern-day "Buck." He was aggressive, violent, destructive, hypersexual, and animalistic, referring to himself as the wolf and saying, *"King Kong ain't got nothing on me."* He also displayed total power over his fellow white detective. Ultimately, the character was killed in the film, which is represented as deserving of the "Buck" character. Denzel Washington was awarded an Academy Award for Best Actor. However, in my humble opinion, his best acting performance was in the 1987 film Cry Freedom, where he played Stephen Biko, the South African anti-apartheid activist.

In 2001, in the film "Monster's Ball," a Black American woman, Leticia Musgrove, which Halle Berry played, portrayed the modern-day "Jezebel with a sprinkle of Welfare Queen." She was lustful, enticing, temping, seductive, hypersexual, mooched off the welfare system, and had a fair complexion with European features. Halle Berry was the first Black American woman to win the Academy Award for Best Actress.

In 2011, in the film "The Help," a Black American woman, Albileen Clark, who was played by Viola Davis, portrayed the modern-day "Mammy" character as a rough, sassy, argumentative, and loyal servant. The movie centers around Southern white privilege in the 1960s in Mississippi. A young white woman who wanted to become a writer interviews the Black American maids and learns of the ill-treatment they have experienced as maids from their white employers. She eventually writes a book in the end. Viola Davis was nominated for the Academy Award for Best Actress for her role in this film.

Another popular character I forgot to mention is the "Magical Negro." This character is portrayed as having some mystical powers, being subservient to their white counterpart, living an unimportant life, and merely existing to help their white co-characters whenever they are in crisis by ignoring their own lives and routines. This character exists in both male and female Black American roles. Magical Negroes are nothing less than problematic because they have no desires of their own. They exist in movies as supporting characters for the white lead. Reinforcing the stereotype that Black Americans don't live a valuable life, as though they do not require intricate storylines of their own because their lives don't matter, is the propaganda promoted by such movies. There have been many Magical Negroes films produced.

In the 1979 film, 'The Black Stallion,' Clarence Muse plays the character of Snoe. The discomforting cliché is portrayed in the character of Snoe as the Magical Negro imagined by a white storyteller in the form of a fantasy. Snoe has magical and strange intuitive powers, yet only exists as an imaginary friend outside of the integral role that was obviously offered to his white counterpart.

In the 1990 film Ghost, Oda Mae Brown, who has psychic powers, is played by Whoopi Goldberg. Her main purpose was to protect the white female character Molly by spiritually connecting with her deceased husband Sam to aid in protecting Molly from the men who killed Sam.

In the 1999 film "The Green Mile," Michael Clarke Duncan portrayed the character of John Coffey, a massive Black American man on death row for raping and killing two white girls who happened to possess a mystical skill to heal others by touching them. John used his skills to benefit white people and asked for nothing in return.

In the 2000 film "Legend of Bagger Vance," Will Smith portrayed the character of Bagger Vance, a mysterious traveler who caddies for a white golfer and teaches him how to golf like a pro and once again asks for nothing in return. His sole purpose was to please the white character.

The more an actor/actress can resemble the anti-Black characters created by the Hollywood film and television industry, which reaffirms the perceived realism of Black Americans in the psyche of the dominant white culture, the more they are rewarded with accolades from the industry.

A similar negative anti-Black image was also portrayed through the characters depicting Black Americans in animated cartoons in the early to mid-20th century, which were marketed to American children.

'Hittin' the Trail for Hallelujah Land' (1931) is a Merrie Melodies cartoon by Warner Bros. It portrayed a blackface caricature of an African-American character that was animal-like in its nature. Uncle Tom was a character living in slavery in the Southern regions. Piggy and Fluffy had jet-black skin with white snouts, depicting them as pigs. The pigs wore fine clothing, while Uncle Tom wore ragged clothes— further reiterating the idea that he was a happy slave.

In the cartoon, Tom and Jerry, in Plane Dumb (1932), the characters spoke of how they would not be safe in Africa and proceeded to disguise themselves by painting their faces black. After that, they are suddenly shown to speak incorrect English, saying sentences like, "Is we in Africa?" And not just that, but the portrayal of native Black people was nothing less than cannibalistic. Aggressive men wearing bones in their hair wanted the two main white characters out of their region at any cost. Cartoons like this ensured that racism existed even within the boundaries of shows that were child-oriented. Which in turn shaped the psyche of even children about how they should perceive Black Americans.

In Fantasia: 'The Pastoral Symphony,' the 1940 Disney film portrayed a scene with a Sunflower centaur, who was a servant for all the other characters in the movie. Other centaurs in the movie were half-human horses, while Sunflower was a black centaur with a donkey's body where the horse part should have been. The film also showed a scene where Sunflower polished the hooves of her white-centaur counterpart, acting sloppy and giddy compared to the other centaurs. Eventually, Disney took the scene out of the other versions of the film in the late 1960s.

Released in 1941, "Dumbo" was introduced as a Disney story of an abandoned elephant. Everything appeared to be progressing smoothly until the crows unexpectedly made their entrance in the film. The main crow is known as Jim Crow, and this group of crows would sing and talk in Jive language.

In the recent news released by Disney, when they announced the remake of "That Little Mermaid," they revealed that they were about to cast a Black American to play the character of Ariel; this sparked huge racist backlash from the white fans who thought that diversifying the main character of the show would completely diminish the movie's storyline. This can be taken as another example that portrays how American society, along with the film industry, has shaped the inflated psyche of white Americans.

Apart from using movies and TV shows, other art forms have also been used to perpetuate anti-Blackness. The rap music entertainment industry has morphed into Black negativity, and Black rap artists are perpetuating the negativity by degrading the Black woman, calling her a b*tch or h*e, glorifying violence/killing one another, and focusing on colorism/hair texture within the Black community.

Despite certain advancements in the Hollywood film/television industry, the persistence of Black American stereotypes remains prevalent, extending their influence on a global scale. For example, when I ask friends/associates who immigrated to the United States about their perceptions of Black Americans before they arrived in the United States, the consistent responses are usually similar, "Black Americans are dangerous, drug dealers/users, criminals, uneducated, and dependent on welfare." I am also told that they are warned not to associate with Black Americans. When I ask what shaped your perception, the consistent response is "American news," "movies," and "television shows."

Television, big-screen cinema, music, and social media are vehicles used without most people being aware of how their psyches are shaped to accept the dominant narrative of disproportionately negative portrayals of Black Americans and favorable portrayals of whites. In my opinion, all of this is done by a small group of people in authority over these mediums, through which they reach such a large number of people without their knowledge of what their minds are being fed by these mediums.

My attempt in this whole analysis is to show how Hollywood disproportionately portrays negative perceptions of Black Americans and overwhelmingly shows favorable perceptions of whites. However, this is not just something that was done in the distant past; it continues to this day. The negative anti-Black characters are just adjusted to adapt to the current times and are viewed by audiences worldwide. If you consistently show people in a negative light, people will start to believe it, which has been done since the industry's inception in the United States.

To conclude this chapter, I would like to share a thought-provoking quote from Chimamanda Ngozi Adichie, who so elegantly stated in her 2009 TED Talk presentation, "The Danger of a Single Story."

"The consequence of the single story being told over and over about a people - It robs people of dignity, it makes our recognition of our equal humanity difficult, and it emphasizes how we are different rather than how we are similar."[35]

---

[35] Adichie, Chimamanda, N. (2014). *The danger of a single story* [Video]. TED Talks. https://www.ted.com/talks/chimamanda_ngozi_adichie_the_danger_of_a_single_story/c

Chapter 4
Inflated Psyche – White Superiority Complex

Racism is a system of race-based advantage, providing privileges to only one group; a social construct created by man. It is the longest-enduring pandemic in U.S. history, with no holistic approach initiated by the U.S. government to eradicate this devastating illness. Rather racism is deeply ingrained within the U.S. psyche, and it is virtually impossible to escape.

As I mentioned in chapter one, the ratification of the U.S. Constitution in 1788 established the governance and social structure of the newly colonized United States. Two years later, the Nationality Act of 1790 limited United States citizenship to "whites" only immigrants, and "white" preferences remained until the 1965 Immigration and Nationality Act. Today, it is crucial to recognize and comprehend how the American psyche was shaped and how white Americans developed this inflated psyche. White Americans grew up in a society where maintaining the social order of white superiority was paramount by imposing laws and restrictions on Black Americans, forbidding them from enjoying the simple pleasures of life and basic human rights.

The consequences of a social construct based upon racial classification and segregation inevitably shaped the psyche of white Americans to believe, consciously or semi-consciously, that they are the only race worthy of being privileged members of society. The result is only natural; Living in a society emphasizing a racial and social order makes most people adhere to it and normalize the practice; it becomes a reality in their subconscious. In this chapter, I will explore how this inflated psyche manifests itself in society.

Politicians, policymakers, powerful individuals, and institutions assuage their guilt and justify or hide their lack of action to eradicate the woes of systemic racism and its continued impact on American society by projecting it as an ugly facet of the dark ages. Tying the neat albeit horrible knot of the era of chattel slavery onto it, and refusing to acknowledge how it's ever-present nature in the life of every American citizen continues to affect the way Black Americans are perceived in this country today. This enables the powers that be to move the focus from their inaction thus placating the public with a false sense of progress.

When in reality, racist ideas are still deeply embedded in the hearts and minds of white Americans and continue to drive their actions in everyday life.

Sadly, only minimal efforts are directed toward eradicating the problem of the white superiority complex from its root. While delving deep into studying the issue of white superiority, I have observed that in the medical profession, specifically mental health literature, the focus on practical interventions to address this issue by applying multifaceted, multicultural, and social justice counseling strategies is of negligible concern.

Another aspect of society that reflects the white superiority complex is the fact that white Americans disproportionately influence or hold most of the powerful positions in this country, be it a government, private or non-profit.

However, all these problems are deeply rooted in many more complex issues that will be revealed in this chapter. Studying and experiencing racism, I have observed many of the adverse consequences on both white and non-white citizens, inflicted in the form of actions by white Americans innocently helping to sustain a societal status quo that continues to maintain racialized arrangements in the structural hierarchy of the United States which continues to the detriment of Black Americans while privileging white Americans.

White Savior Complex

Helping others does not always indicate that the person who is helping is addressing the direct causation of the problem. In most cases, helping makes that person feel good about themselves. Sometimes the efforts to help others are threaded with ulterior motives, and such motives are defined by the term White Savior Complex. The term explains how white people constantly feel the need to help non-white citizens because of their inflated psyche; they believe that they are the sole authority in helping others and that they are of higher intelligence than non-white citizens. This behavior indicates the reinforcement of the long-held belief of white Americans that white genes are superior to others and thus should be respected.

The unfortunate fact about these beliefs is that even if most white citizens do not believe they are superior, they still exhibit the traits common to White Savior Complex. The reason at large is that they have consciously or semi-consciously accepted and believed in the social order of white superiority since the inception of the United States. It is so deeply embedded within the system that now it is difficult to separate it from what is considered normal. The prejudice enacted through all the institutions, has painted a picture in the minds of the American people that Black Americans are inferior and white Americans are superior, and the psyche has accepted it as reality.

Many people enacting the white savior complex might think their actions challenge discrimination, but in contrast, it emphasizes inequity. I believe the only way to eradicate this problem is to understand how deeply rooted it is and that it would take proper and collective introspection to eliminate it. Knowing the story of colonialism should be enough reason to curb it from the root, for this practice has many drastic consequences that have been evident throughout the years

White Fragility

A sociologist, Robin DeAngelo, coined the term "white fragility," which refers to white people's responses to discussions involving addressing systemic racism. While working as a diversity trainer in different workplaces, she encountered many similar experiences whenever the topic of racism was discussed. Such behaviors are commonly witnessed in workplaces, schools, and even in political settings where it is crucial to address the issues of racism to come up with better and more efficient ways to get rid of it. Since the representative positions are only held by white citizens, the progress of curbing the issue of prejudice has also been slowed down. In fact, it wouldn't be wrong to say that little to no efforts have been made to deal with this major issue that affects many of the citizens in this country.

The book "*White Fragility*" written by Robin DiAngelo, describes the elements of the term as denial, refusing to acknowledge the problems of racism, or entirely avoiding the discussion about racism. (DiAngelo) This explains the low racial tolerance of white citizens and how they choose anger, silence, and other defensive moves to avoid racial stress.[36]

People are parts of what society constitutes as a whole, which is why they cannot address the instances of discrimination that have been normalized without analyzing their environment with a critical approach—without realizing most of the people are driven by white supremacist ideas, and an active intent to do so. This is to say that most of the population would have to unlearn what they have been taught as normal to get a perspective of what is happening around them. Their idea of normal has been molded to the extent that most unconsciously act according to systemic racism.

White Privilege

Privilege is hard to acknowledge for those who are born with it. For them, it is as normal as water to fish or air to birds. White privilege refers to the benefits and rights granted to those who, by the social construct of race, look like those dominating the powerful positions in American institutions. These people are given resources and access to power for positions and situations that are unavailable to people of

---

[36]Di Angelo, Robin (2018). *White Fragility: Why it's So Hard for White People to Talk About Racism. Beacon Press.*

color. However, if a person of color rises to power, the influence of "the white powers that be" ensure that they adhere to the social order of white superiority, indicating that how a human being is treated largely depends on their skin color.

Again, most of the white population are aware of the privileges they have been granted as they matriculate through life. Still, the American people must understand that the long-standing system only benefits a certain group of people and this is intentional.

Decisions made by the people in power, whether in politics, business, or social settings, affect white Americans very differently than Black Americans. History is witness to instances of the purposeful construction of the systemic structure that endows white citizens with privileges and withholds those same privileges from Black Americans.

White privilege allows white citizens to adhere to the practices of systemic racism consciously. Therefore, if anti-Black policies/laws do not affect them personally, they intentionally or unintentionally toe the line. This is how the system has been intentionally crafted to undermine a specific group of individuals. These dynamics have persisted since the very beginning, leading people to perceive them as the norm. The problem still exists in society because every individual is taught to only fend for themselves, which instigates the need to ignore all around. There is no sense of oneness or unity as in the "United" States of America.

White Supremacy

White supremacy has existed since the advent of the United States, manifesting in different forms throughout the years, with not enough serious work done to identify the causes or eradicating its wide and long-lasting spread in the United States. However, some work has been done recently through the examination of academic history textbooks that have dominated academia for years. To get to the root of this, one must first, realize that - the academic textbook industry is controlled by a majority white individuals, and the history taught is from a white perspective, not grounded in complete truth. These books are like a virus, extremely contagious, spreading untruths to the minds of generations of American schoolchildren in an effort to build Democratic institutions and values that profit those in power for the sole purpose of maintaining that power endowed to the dominant white culture. This can also be considered one of the reasons why people don't see the problem clearly today; they have never been exposed to it thoroughly. Reading the history and the atrocities Black Americans have faced would give the citizens a clear idea of what activities have been practiced in the past and are very much part of the present reality facing Black Americans. This approach would afford chances to reflect on their actions and those of others and lay the foundation for initiatives focused to eliminate the problem at its root.

It is commonly believed that the portrayal of white supremacy is only done by imposing laws and policies. However, its long-lasting standing throughout the years is molded into the fabric of the American lifestyle. As a result, most white people maintain it daily and consciously realize it, yet are in denial of individual racism. For instance, the white savior complex is often performed by white citizens with the intention of helping their non-white fellow citizens. However, their actions never address systemic racism, which is the root cause of the problems. Therefore, the impact of their actions is rooted in white supremacy, which still has a damaging impact on society.

One deceptive misconception that is widely held by the majority is that only white people exude and support white supremacy. It is the most damaging because it withholds Black Americans and other non-whites from critically examining their own behavior that might be contributing to it. It is an act of the psyche aligning with whiteness and perpetuating white supremacy consciously, semi-consciously, or unconsciously for status and greed. This is the approach that the current situation requires everyone to adopt; to examine our behaviors and find out in what ways we are contributing to the problem as well.

To sum it up, white supremacy in the United States is no surprise or accident at all. However, to rid this nation of this illness, it will take a collective of conscious minds that are painfully aware and willing to put in the actual work to eradicate this long-running contagious virus. We must undertake these efforts for the sake of future generations. The racism that has long existed in American society has been deeply embedded in every institution. such as education, criminal justice, housing, banking, healthcare, etc. In the past and present, Black Americans have been intentionally excluded or held limited roles of influence/leadership across the institutions mentioned above. As previously discussed, when Black Americans ascend to influential/leadership roles, they also adhere to the social order of white supremacy. The contributing factors for this are the governmental anti-Black policies, the long institution of chattel slavery, the Jim Crow segregation Era, and systemic racism that still exists today. All that has inked the pages of history remains deeply embedded within the system and lifestyle of the United States.

Housing

The housing discrimination policies enacted in the twentieth century at the federal, state, and local levels restricted where Black Americans could live and, in many cases, prevented Black Americans from homeownership. This ensured that the majority of Black Americans were entrapped in poverty through the segregation enacted through the division of geography. This sort of systemic racism created a vicious cycle of generational poverty for many without an escape route and is one of the contributing reasons for the staggering wealth disparity between whites and Blacks in this country today.

Redlining in banking was another way through which local and federal governments created systemic inequity for Black American communities across the U.S. The practice started in the 1930s when lenders drew red lines on maps to outline the parts of the city they would not loan to; those mainly included the Black communities.

Even though the 1968 Fair Housing Act made it illegal to redline, it still affects the Black community today. Specifically, when it comes to home value, for example, comparison of the same exact home, design, and developer, one in a predominantly white neighborhood and the other in a predominantly Black neighborhood, there will be a stark difference in price and equity. People might like to believe that redlining does not exist anymore, but it is still persistent in many areas where the services/value that citizens are provided are according to whether they are Black or white.

In his book "The Color of Law," Richard Rothstein explains that there are separate neighborhoods for Black Americans and Whites due to government policies. Federal, local, and state governments implemented policies/laws that confined Black Americans to secluded areas without basic facilities, which continued to impact every aspect of their lives, from educational, and job opportunities to economic well-being and physical health.[37]

Banking

Throughout the history of the United States, discrimination in the financial industry has been apparent. Following emancipation in 1865, the Freedmen's Savings Bank was established to help newly freed former enslaved Black Americans establish savings accounts. However, after many former enslaved Black Americans had deposited their hard-earned money in the Freedmen's Savings Bank, the mismanagement and fraud by the board of directors weakened the foundation of the bank, and one particular businessman, Henry D. Cook, a close friend of then President Ulysses S. Grant, was appointed first Governor of the District of Columbia (1871 – 1873), by President Ulysses S. Grant, utilized the money from the Freedmen's Bank to invest in his quarry operations. Cook's quarry business went belly-up because he could not pay his debts, which caused the Freedmen's Savings Bank to go bankrupt in 1876.

---

[37]Rothstein, Richard. (2018). *The Color of Law: A Forgotten History of How Our Government Segregated America.* Liveright Publishing Corporation, New York.

The closing of the bank devastated the formerly enslaved Black American community. Tens of thousands collectively lost their hard-earned savings, estimated at the time as over $3 million. Many of the former enslaved Black Americans believed the federal government would protect them. However, only about half of the depositors received only about three-fifths of the value of their accounts, and others received nothing. The federal government investigated, but Henry D. Cook and his conspirators were never indicted, and no one was ever held responsible for stealing the hard-earn savings from the former enslaved Black Americans. Henry D. Cook lived out his life without a bother until his death. This one incident is one great example of the story of white privilege. The failure of the Freedmen's Savings Bank began the legacy of racism in the banking industry for Black Americans.[38]

Criminal Justice

The American criminal justice system has been disproportionately targeting Black Americans since the ratification of the U.S. Constitution, starting with (Article IV, Section 2, Clause 2). This was known as the "Fugitive Slave Clause." It basically states that if an "African Slave" escapes to another state, that state must return the fugitive "African Slave" to the state from which the "African Slave" came.

---

[38]Washington, Reginald. (2022). *The Freedman's Savings and Trust Company and African American*. National Archives.
https://www.archives.gov/publications/prologue/1997/summer/freedmans-savings-and-trust.html

After emancipation, white Southern legislators enacted "Black Code" laws across the Southern United States, which allowed local authorities to arrest Black Americans for minor infractions and sentenced them to the convict leasing system. This allowed the State to lease the prisoner out to a plantation/farm or private company, and the state would receive a profit, but the prisoner would earn nothing. The prisoner would be forced to perform this work under dangerous and deadly conditions. Once again, Black Americans were overwhelmingly targeted. In the early 1900s, convict leasing ended and was replaced by chain gang labor, again with no monetary compensation.

Douglas Blackmon's book "Slavery by Another Name: The Re-Enslavement of Black Americans from the Civil War to World War II" shines the light on how Blacks were arrested and charged with excessive fines, with no means to pay those bizarre fines.[39] Blacks were sold as forced laborers to coal mines, quarries, railroads, lumber camps, and farm plantations.

An added layer of the American criminal justice system's institutionalized racism concerns the Violent Crime Control and Law Enforcement Act of 1994. This entailed Congress authorizing billions of dollars for states to build more prisons and increase the hiring of local and state police officers. This gave birth to a prison system driven by profit and coupled with harsh crime policies, which resulted in the mass incarceration of targeted Black Americans serving lengthy prison sentences for nonviolent crimes. In other words, Black

---

[39]Blackmon, Douglas A. (2008). *Slavery by Another Name: The Re-Enslavement of Black Americans from the Civil War to World War II. Anchor Books, A Division of Random House, Inc. New York*

communities were over-policed, disproportionately targeted, arrested, charged, convicted, and sent to prison for crimes that most whites would get a slap on the wrist for committing. This continued discriminatory incarceration of Black Americans has left a gap in the Black family household that further destabilizes the Black communities, and the effect is still felt today.

Michelle Alexander's book "The New Jim Crow" explains how the Violent Crime Control and Law Enforcement Act of 1994 created dozens of new federal capital crimes and authorized more than $16 billion for state prison grants and state and local police expansion forces. The Act also included a "three strikes, and you're out" law that mandated 25-year to life sentences for nonviolent felonies such as a prior petty thief offense.[40]

Education

Institutionally sanctioned white supremacy can be termed as the foundation of the United States, and racism as its manifestation. For instance, all educational/academic accreditation and curriculums are controlled to a large extent by white individuals. As I mentioned in chapter two, the history of the American educational system was steeped in anti-Blackness by white racial actors.

The desegregation of children in public schools following the ruling in the 1954 Supreme Court case "Brown v. Board of Education of Topeka" was important. However, it sparked outrage among many white Americans, especially in the Southern States, and many Black

---

[40] Alexander, Michelle. (2012). *The New Jim Crow: Mass Incarceration in the Age of Colorblindness.* The New Press, New York.

American teachers who were great educators and cared deeply about educating Black American students were fired or demoted. Most were replaced by white teachers, expecting low achievement from Black American kids, and perceiving that they did not have the innate ability to do rigorous academic work and were just passed through the system. This led to different expectations for particular racial groups. This perception is still prevalent today in the public school system.

Healthcare

Throughout the history of the United States, in the healthcare/medical profession, racism has been prevalent toward Black Americans. For example, Black bodies were exploited throughout the 19th and 20th centuries for the development of U.S. medical studies and experiments.

As mentioned in chapter one, James Marion Sims, an American physician, performed vaginal experiments on enslaved Black women without their consent and without anesthesia. After the experiments, he developed surgical techniques to repair the fistula. He was credited as the "father of gynecology," and today, we read about Dr. Sims in books without the mention of these women who suffered from inhumane treatment.

Another infamous and gruesome incident in the history of medicine was the Tuskegee Syphilis Experiment. In 1932 the Tuskegee Syphilis Experiment was conducted by the United States Public Health Service (USPHS), which did not collect informed consent from the participants; the Black American men involved in the study were lied to by the researchers and not offered the treatment to cure them. The study's goal was to observe the natural history of untreated syphilis in the black population. This experiment was conducted over the course of four decades in Tuskegee. As a result of this experiment, one hundred and twenty-eight participants died of syphilis, forty wives were infected, and nineteen children were born with congenital syphilis. The experiment finally ended in 1972 after Congress passed the National Research Act to prevent human exploitation in research. Not a single person was prosecuted for the violations, deaths, and injuries caused by the experiment. The federal government did not launch any formal apology to the victims and their families.[41]

These infamous experiments not only portray the harsh reality of discrimination against Black Americans but also represent how the American Medical Association (AMA) code of ethics was ignored and medical procedures were misused without any consequences.

Going back in time can lead us to find myriad examples of discrimination in the field of medicine and healthcare in the United States that portray the mistreatment of Black Americans. But to call them historical structures would be wrong, for these practices still exist to this day. Addressing the issues of discrimination, segregation, racism, and other systemic barriers in the healthcare system must emerge to effectively promote and provide citizens' equity.

---

[41]McVean, Ada. (2019). *40 Years of Human Experimentation in America: The Tuskegee Study*. Office for Science and Society. https://www.mcgill.ca/oss/article/history/40-years-human-experimentation-america-tuskegee-study

Furthermore, after years of segregation by medical professionals and the struggle to fight to mitigate it, it can be concluded that all the efforts had been in vain, for it still has not ceased to exist.

In 2005 National Academy of Medicine (NAM) published a report that documented, "lower quality health care that Black Americans were provided was the major factor of deteriorating health issues in the Black community. It is also noted that through the results of several studies, it was revealed that Black patients were less likely to be provided with coronary bypass and angiography and were given cheaper, older, and more conservative treatments than white citizens.[42]

Another study titled '*Black Americans are Systematically Under-Treated for Pain. Why?*' published by the University of Virginia revealed that healthcare professionals are significantly less likely to prescribe pain medication to Black patients. If prescribed, the doses are lower than that of white patients. The reason mentioned in this study for this racial disparity being perpetrated by healthcare professionals was due to the belief they held of Black Americans, which implied that Black people experience less pain. I can't make this stuff up! This might be hard to believe as doctors are expected to never discriminate among their patients, but perhaps hatred knows no limits.[43]

---

[42]Bridges, Khiara, M. (n.d.). *Implicit Bias and Racial Disparities in Health Care*. https://www.americanbar.org/groups/crsj/publications/human_rights_magazine_home/the-state-of-healthcare-in-the-united-states/racial-disparities-in-health-care/

[43]Trawalter, Sophie. (2020). *Black Americans are Systematically Under-Treated for Pain. Why?* Frank Batten School of Leadership and Public Policy | University of Virginia. https://batten.virginia.edu/about/news/black-americans-are-systematically-under-treated-pain-why

The hypothesis in the article determined that an individual's belief in the biological roots of race can contribute to their perception of Black Americans' pain tolerance. Another interesting fact denotes how modern society still indulges in the false perception that a Black person's body is biologically different from that of a white person. This illustrates how the American psyche has been shaped into perceiving Black Americans as different from the white population, even in this age, when many people are educated and can form well-informed opinions about everything.

The tragic reality is that the American psyche has been molded into the agenda of discrimination to the extent that people now perform it unconsciously throughout their day-to-day life. The most recent instance of this was during the Covid-19 pandemic. The mortality rate for Black Americans contracting the virus was higher than any other ethnic group in this county. This is a clear example of the ongoing inequalities tied to the Black community and access to high-quality healthcare. As the stats of people affected by the virus were reviewed with consideration of factors such as race, gender, age, class, and medical history, it was deduced that minorities had been disproportionately impacted by the pandemic.

According to a study, even though during the outbreak of Covid-19, all fifty states were provided with the testing kits, the results gathered appeared to have inconsistencies.[44] For instance, in Kansas, 94,780 tests were conducted, of which only 4,854 were from Black

---

[44]Vasquez Reyes, Maritza. "The Disproportional Impact of COVID-19 on African Americans." Health and Human Rights, vol. 22, no. 2, 1 Dec. 2020, pp. 299–307, www.ncbi.nlm.nih.gov/pmc/articles/PMC7762908/#:~:text=Approximately%2097.9%20ou t%20of%20every.

Americans and 50,070 were from whites. But almost a third of the state's Covid-19 deaths were of Black citizens. All in all, the study showed how even among all the other ethnic groups, Black Americans especially had been most affected by Covid19.

There have been, however, recently some improvements in academic medicine by incorporating the courses highlighting the awareness of the health care inequities. However, despite these recent changes, it can be said that fair treatment of all human beings, regardless of the color of their skin, will take some time.

It can be concluded that systemic racism in the healthcare system is still, to this day, well documented, which ultimately impacts the entire health journey for Black citizens.

In the final analysis, throughout American history, the discourse of race has been frequently at the forefront. Contrary to popular belief among white Americans, racism still prevails in every aspect of American life. Whether consciously or semi-consciously, the white inflated psyche has been consistent and, as a collective, has never combatted or addressed this systemic problem holistically or with a critical eye. The only difference in modern times is that racism is not as overt in its presentation. Nonetheless, it is still very much a part of society; The problem persists in the invisibility of whiteness.

Chapter 5
Scattered Psyche

After emancipation and the continued oppression and suffering, Black Americans consciously, semi-consciously, or unconsciously accepted a covenant with the social structure of white superiority in the hope of reciprocity that has yet to come to fruition. This covenant has been detrimental in the sense that it required Black Americans to continuously prove themselves to the social structure of white superiority for acceptance by forming their identities in a manner that was considered normal to their standards.

Dr. W.E.B. Du Bois dubbed it as 'double consciousness' in his 1903 book 'The Souls of Black Folks.' He writes, "*The Negro is a sort of the seventh son, born with a veil, and gifted with second-sight in the American world, a world which yields him no true self-consciousness, but only lets him see himself through the revelation of the other world. It is a peculiar sensation, this double consciousness, this sense of always looking at oneself through the eyes of others, of measuring one's soul by the tape of a world that looks on in amused contempt and pity. One ever feels his two-ness, an American, a Negro; two souls, two thoughts, two unreconciled strivings; two warring ideals in one dark body, whose dogged strength alone keeps it from being torn asunder.*"[45]

He spent his extensive career trying to understand the socio-historic conditions and their impact on the people most affected by

---

[45]Du Bois, W.E.B. (PhD) (2003). *The Souls of Black Folk.* Barnes & Noble Classics, New York – First published in 1903.

them, especially how the social environment of the United States has affected Black Americans.

When an individual is devoid of all the rights to define his identity, they tend to adopt the ideas others have of them and then define themselves as such. The discourse throughout the United States has vigorously defined the image of Black Americans on how to perceive themselves. When you give others the power to define you then you lose the essence of your personality and identity, which leads to your personality merging into several pieces beyond your comprehension and eventually becoming the fragments defined as acceptable in your society.

Since then, there have been many others who have written books/articles addressing this topic.

In "The Souls of Black Folk," published in 2003 by Barnes & Noble Classics with the introduction notes by Farah Jasmine Griffin, she writes, *"Double consciousness defines a psychological sense experienced by African Americans whereby they possess a national identity, 'an American,' within a nation that despises their racial identity, 'a Negro.' It also refers to the ability of Black Americans to see themselves only through the eyes of white Americans, to measure their intelligence, beauty, and sense of self-worth by standards set by others."*[46]

---

[46]Du Bois, W.E.B. (PhD) (2003). *The Souls of Black Folk.* Barnes & Noble Classics, New York – First published in 1903.

Dr. Bobby E. Wright introduced the theory of 'Mentacide' in 1978. This theory is defined as the *"deliberate act and systematic destruction of an individual or group's mind."*[47]

In Dr. Joy DeGruy, 2005 book "Post Traumatic Slave Syndrome: America's Legacy of Enduring Injury and Healing," she introduced the theory of Post-Traumatic Slave Syndrome *"a condition that exists when a population has experienced multigenerational trauma resulting from centuries of slavery and continues to experience oppression and institutionalized racism today."*[48]

As I mentioned in the previous chapters, Black Americans have endured great challenges to obtain basic human rights in this nation. This deliberate and systematic treatment has caused extreme human suffering and trauma, impacting Black Americans' psyche as a collective. The psyche of Black Americans consciously, semi-consciously, or unconsciously perpetuates racist ideologies and beliefs in the Black community today which have contributed enormously to shaping the scattered psyche of Black Americans as a whole. Let me be clear, I am speaking from a Black American collective perspective, not from a generalization perspective.

There was a moment in the history of this nation when it appeared that Black Americans as a collective were moving in the right direction in terms of collective consciousness, specifically, a collective uplift in the Black American community.

---

[47]Wright, Bobby. (PhD) (1978) *"Mentacide: The Ultimate Threat to The Black Race."* pp. 1-15.

[48]Degruy, Joy (PhD) (2005). *Post Traumatic Slave Syndrome: America's legacy of Enduring Injury & Healing.* Uptone Press.

The Black Power Movement in the '60s was a moment of Black collective consciousness/uplift in the Black community. The Black Power Movement was about institution building, such as schools – educating the community on accurate Black American history. Healthcare clinics, ambulance services, food cooperatives, farms, and other small community businesses flourished until the turmoil/pushback from the federal government and the movement failed to keep its momentum. Although the movement was short-lived, it was a time when Blacks collectively celebrated their authentic Black beauty and appreciated their true authentic selves. Though I was only a little kid, I had three older sisters, and I would enjoy watching them, and their friends appreciate the natural beauty of the different afros styles and listening to James Brown's on the record player, singing "Say It Loud – I'm Black and I'm Proud."

This chapter will focus on the impact of this cruel treatment, how it scattered the psyche of Black Americans as a collective, and how it still manifests itself in society today. A scattered psyche can be defined as a distracted and disorganized mindset rather than naturally working together as a collective.

Let me reiterate, I am not a psychologist, sociologist, or psychiatrist. I am just a Black man with lived experience in the Black community in this country. I speak on behalf of what I have experienced, seen, and read regarding the treatment Black Americans have experienced throughout history, which continues to haunt the community even today.

The reason for analyzing the whole structure of the society that we live in was purely based on the intention to make people aware of what they have been unconsciously participating in for years without their knowledge because it has been instilled within us with years of functioning.

Consumerism

After integration and the passage of the 1964 civil rights Bill, Black Americans no longer concerned themselves with collective community uplift. It was every man for him/herself mentality. It is natural to disperse from a collective objective when you feel threatened by the majority that is in power.

Not being accustomed to moving around freely without consequences and being able to shop at establishments that were prohibited in the past, Black Americans started indulging in the everyday activities that they were shunned from earlier. They took this opportunity as a chance to merge themselves into a society where they were not accepted formally.

Therefore, they started to spend all their hard-earned money outside of the Black community and neglected the Black-owned businesses in their community, causing most of the Black American businesses to go bust. All of this was done for the sole purpose of wanting to feel accepted and have a sense of belonging in a community that despised them, without the awareness of the detrimental effects it was causing on their community. The hatred that the dominant white culture has been emitting toward Black Americans still shows its effects by the efforts Black people put into trying to be accepted by the social structure of white supremacy.

When I was a young kid, my uncle would tell me the story about "The Black-owned icehouse store (where blocks of ice were sold) that went out of business because Black Americans in the community believed that the white-owned icehouse store sold colder ice."

Maybe it was just a metaphor, explaining to me that Black Americans believed that white-owned businesses were better, as this is what had always been taught: whites are better in every aspect of American life.

Money circulation is the part of the economy that is physically utilized to act on transactions between businesses and consumers. This is the money that is stored in banking institutions. This process makes money circulation an important characteristic of a community's potential for economic mobility because more money circulation means higher financial stability and the potential for economic growth in the community.

Today, money circulates only once in the Black American community. The *Selig Center for Economic Growth* published in their study that "money circulates one time in the Black American community, six times in the Latino community, and nine times in the Asian community. In the white community, money circulates an unlimited number of times."[49]

Black Americans are considered the second largest consumer group in this country, with $1.4 trillion in spending power as a

---

[49] How dollars circulate in Black Communities, *Greenwood*. (2021).
https://gogreenwood.com/how-dollars-circulate-in-black-communities/

collective. That is more than most developed nations. Yet money only circulates once in the Black American community.[50]

With 47.8 million members, Black Americans are the second-largest consumer group, representing a $300 billion market opportunity for companies. According to McKinsey, while comprising 13.4% of the U.S. population, Black households spent just under 10% of the nation's total on goods and services in 2019.

In 2019, Black households spent around $835 billion on consumer goods, climbing by 5% yearly over the preceding decade. However, most of that $835 billion was spent outside of the Black American community.[51]

Black Americans also, as a collective, spend exorbitant amounts of money on luxury consumer goods. Whether it is for status, to make them feel important, or keeping up with the Joneses, which makes them happy, makes them feel relevant within society, or the reason could be that they just have disposable income and just want to splurge. The psychological reason behind this spending is not the point. The point is that most of this money is spent outside of the Black community, which can be determined as the major reason why the Black community is lagging in the aspect of financial stability.

---

[50]Hale, Kori. (2021, September 17). The $300 Billion Black American Consumerism Bag Breeds Big Business Opportunities. *Forbes*.
https://www.forbes.com/sites/korihale/2021/09/17/the-300-billion-black-american-consumerism-bag-breeds-big-business-opportunities/?sh=7c976dd434fc

[51]Chui, Michael. Gregg, Brian. Kohli, Sajal. and Stewart, Shelly. (2021). *A $300 billion opportunity: Serving the emerging Black American consumer*. (2021, August 6). McKinsey & Company. https://www.mckinsey.com/featured-insights/diversity-and-inclusion/a-300-billion-dollar-opportunity-serving-the-emerging-black-american-consumer

Undoubtedly, this factor significantly contributes to the wealth disparity between Black and white communities. However, another major key factor is the years of neglect and underinvestment by the private sector that has deprived most Black communities of shopping options and essential services due to the lack of development. As long as Black Americans are willing to go outside of their communities for consumer items without demanding investments and development as a collective in Black American communities, nothing will change. As I mentioned earlier, this behavior pattern started after integration and the passage of the 1964 civil rights Bill. Not accustomed to shopping at places that once did not want their business because of their skin color. It appears that, as a collective, Black Americans have normalized this behavior at the expense of neglecting the Black American community's growth. Today, most Black American communities in this nation suffer from limited access to fresh and healthy food options and quality medical care.

We go to school, work hard, attain great careers, move out of the Black community, and become assimilated by taking on the traits of the dominant culture. Then we start to marginalize our communities according to the social structure of white superiority. We let them control us and our actions without realizing the effects it inflicts on our communities.

As a collective, we seem to care less for community uplift and more about personal gain and power, which points our attention toward the issue that we have lost the sense of feeling for others who look like us. We get into the conventional race to achieve bigger goals, to get the next big job, but along the way, we forget about reaching back to uplift our community. We lose our true identity and transform ourselves into the versions of people that the social structure of white supremacy wants us to become.

The key concept to grasp here is that money needs to circulate in the Black community longer, which can be done by Black Americans starting more of their own businesses, supporting current and future Black-owned businesses, reinvesting in the community by buying property, demanding support from community religious leaders, and tangible resources from elected local, state, and federal officials, and not just lip service. Each person has a role to fulfill in achieving this collective goal.

Black preachers should, perhaps, concentrate their effort on establishing an effective, organized Black coalition among the many Black churches/denominations, and focus their energies on institution-building and uplifting the Black community as a collective. Partner with real estate developers to bring retail, office, and public use spaces to the community. The coalition must have comprehensive knowledge/understanding of the U.S. Constitution (the supreme law of the land), politics, accurate Black American history, economics, business, finance, psychology, and sociology. This will prepare them to educate the community and ensure that the coalition/community is mentally equipped by shifting away from subjective voting to objective voting, demanding what you want and need for the community's collective uplift when politicians come to the church grandstanding for your votes. It's time to shift away from the traditional afterlife and prosperity ministry, holding out hope that God will intervene and right the wrongs of the atrocities that the Black American communities have been subjected to for decades.

"Truth comes to us from the past, then, like gold washed down from the mountains." -Carter G. Woodson.

Many Black preachers in the Black community say they were called to preach by a higher spiritual power with a principal focus on the afterlife. This has been the primary focus of the Black church since emancipation, and yet, as a collective, the Black American communities across this nation continue to be marginalized. This focus was taught to the former enslaved Black Americans by their slave owners and has been passed down from generation to generation. Perhaps the slave owners deliberately focused on the afterlife because of the guilt eating away at their conscience for the inhumane and dehumanizing treatment inflicted on the former enslaved Black Americans in the hope of peace and comfort after they transitioned.

You can go into most Black communities across this country today and find a church on every corner of all sizes/denominations, yet less attention and fewer resources continue to be a national problem in these communities. Perhaps it's time to explore an alternative approach, as mentioned above - institution-building, accurate Black American history, and uplifting the Black community as a collective.

Another larger and more significant piece of the puzzle for collective uplift in the Black American communities is the politicians.

Black Americans have made gains in the U.S. Congress. As of 2021, fifty-seven House members and three Senators were Black, and many Black Americans see this representation as a potential component to increase racial equality in the Black community. However, what the Black community needs is equity and true justice, not equality. Black Americans need to stop "putting the cart before the horse." Equality serves everyone the same, regardless of their needs. Equity and genuine justice promote fairness by acknowledging individual circumstances and providing differentiated support based on specific needs, aiming to achieve equitable outcomes. The essential point I want to emphasize is that Black American communities require equity and genuine justice rather than mere equality to address the multitude of challenges Black American communities face. Once equity and genuine justice are established, equality will naturally follow.

Has there been any proposed equity initiatives by any of the fifty-seven House members or three Senators specifically for the Black American communities? I would go as far as to say very little to nothing has been done for equity in the Black American communities, and some of them have been in office for thirty-plus years, and if you look at their constituents' Black American communities, you would be appalled. As I mentioned earlier, most Black American communities in this nation suffer from limited access to fresh and healthy food options and access to quality medical care, which are basic human needs!

Are they more concerned with party politics, individual recognition, money, and staying in office than they are about the collective uplift in the Black community? After analyzing all the factors present in society, I believe there must be a profound rebirth in the thinking of Black elected officials!

The Black community has suffered enough, and the collective desire to fit in by accepting the social structure of white superiority has caused Black Americans to misplace the memory of the past. The focus is on gaining material possessions that we too often mistake for happiness. As a collective, we have been seduced by greed and vanity to the extent that we forget that there is ongoing economic warfare, and our collective communities have been perpetually neglected. Think about it, Black Americans as a collective totaled approximately $835 billion in consumer expenditures in 2019, with $1.4 trillion in spending power as a collective, and money only circulates once in the Black American community. There is something wrong with this picture; clearly, we can write this story anew as a collective, not scattered!

Hair Texture

Slave owners employed terms such as "nappy," "kinky," "bad," and "wooly" to dehumanize the individuals they enslaved and rationalize their dominance and superiority over the former enslaved Black Americans. After years of this treatment, the psyche of the former enslaved Black Americans as a collective started to see their hair as a burden and ultimately accepted the beauty standards set by the social structure of white supremacy, which defined only fair skin and straight hair as beautiful!

The dislike for our natural hair has been passed down for generations. It is common to hear Black Americans use the same dehumanizing terms (nappy, kinky, and bad) to describe one another's hair. There is still a subconscious fixation on viewing straight hair as good hair and tightly curled hair as bad hair in the Black American community.

Dating back to the early 20th century, Madame C.J. Walker was the first Black American female millionaire who promoted and capitalized on this fixation. She made a fortune selling harsh chemical products to straighten Black American women's hair to boost their self-esteem by making them feel beautiful about their appearance.

Black men jumped on the bandwagon of hair straightening in the 1920s through the 1960s. A surge began to indulge in the practice of what was known as the Conk hairstyle. Conk was a corrosive chemical lye that was often mixed with eggs and potatoes and could cause chemical burns to the skin and scalp to straighten hair.

As I mentioned above, there was a brief moment in the '60s when it appeared that Black Americans as a collective were moving in the right direction in terms of collective consciousness, celebrating the natural, authentic beauty of Black people and appreciating their true authentic selves.

Then in the 1980s through the 1990s, the Black community as a collective reverted back to using harsh chemicals to strengthen their hair. This was called "Jheri Curl." Both Black men and women participated in this practice to achieve the look of loose/straight curls.

Using harsh relaxers for hair straightening is still popular among Black women along with straight weaves and straight wigs. A substantial portion of money is spent on these products that do not translate to the circulation of money in the Black community.

In an article shared by Pride Magazine, *'Who Dominates The World's Black Hair Industry?'* According to market research organization Mintel, the black haircare industry is a statistically lucrative business, with $2.7 billion in sales recorded in 2015, and South Korean corporations' control 60–80% of the market, whereas African-Americans make up only 14% of the United States.[52]

Hair discrimination, implicit bias, media propaganda, and de facto policies contribute to this continued straight hair phenomenon of beauty among the Black community. However, the CROWN Act was introduced to Congress in 2021, which stands for "Creating a Respectful and Open World for Natural Hair" it is a law that prohibits race-based hair discrimination, which is the denial of employment and educational opportunities because of hair texture or protective natural hairstyles. As of August 2022, only eighteen states have enacted the CROWN Act into law, and more than half of all states have filed or pre-filed legislation for consideration. About 1 in 10 states have yet to formally examine the CROWN Act.

The good news is there is a conscious movement and support groups of Black women sprouting up across the country encouraging Black women to embrace their natural hair and empowering them with self-love by overcoming the negative perception passed down from generations that tightly curled hair is bad hair, and straight hair is good hair. Black men should also be encouraged to attend these

---

[52]Chibelushi, Wedaeli. (2020). Who Dominates the World's Black Hair Industry? - Pride Magazine. *Pride Magazine - Celebrating the Woman of Colour.* https://www.pridemagazine.com/who-dominates-the-worlds-black-hair-industry/

support groups to learn how to appreciate the natural beauty of the Black woman.

As collective Black women spend excessive effort, time, and money altering or covering their natural textured hair, trying to assimilate to the beauty standards of straight hair set by the social structures of white superiority. Ultimately, it's an individual's choice to do what they want with their hair. However, doing it because the social structure deems your naturally beautiful hair distasteful or because you have internalized the belief that something is wrong with your naturally beautiful hair is psychological. This continuous behavior has been occurring since the early 20th century in the Black community, and perhaps it's time as a collective to embrace the natural hair that grows out of your scalp. If the social structure has a problem with it, then it is time for the social structure's beauty standards to change. Even if for no other reason, let us do it for the sake of the next generation. The time has come to cease concealing our true beauty and embrace authenticity.

Colorism:

From the early 1700s, the social construct of race, categorizing human beings according to skin color and physical features for power and dominance, has been prevalent in the United States. And most people today in this nation have accepted it and are still fixated on the color of one's skin. Even with all the technological advances, we cannot seem to move past this sick ideology.

During the dehumanizing period of chattel slavery in this country. The slave owner would brutalize and rape young Black enslaved females who would give birth to multiracial children of lighter skin. These children would receive preferential treatment for house duties which were less labor intensive, while the darker-skinned children were relegated to the field.

After emancipation, some fairer skin former enslaved Black Americans established colorism societies within the Black American communities—the "Blue Vein Society." Established in the 19th century to maintain a social hierarchy of perceived privilege that came with having fairer skin. Darker-skin former enslaved Black Americans were excluded from these activities, which led to resentment by the darker-skinned former Black Americans.

In the 20th century, the "Brown Paper Bag Test" was another form of colorism discrimination within Black American communities. The test determined the privileges that were to be provided to an individual based on their skin tone by comparing it to a brown paper bag. If a Black American skin tone matched the bag's color or was lighter, you were granted the privilege to join certain social clubs that were denied to Black Americans darker than the paper bag.

The "Blue Vein Society" and the "Brown Paper Bag Test" are examples of how the Black Americans' psyche perpetuated the same anti-Black ideologies and beliefs as their white oppressors, conforming to the social structure of white superiority.

Even in the Black community today, a significant amount of emphasis is put on skin color. Lighter-skinned Blacks are perceived more favorably than darker-skinned Blacks as a collective in the community. Whether consciously, semi-consciously, or unconsciously, this way of being is still very prevalent in the Black community and has been for a very long time as though it's codified into our psyche.

I have witnessed this way of being on many occasions in my life. For example, I was once visiting a friend's housewarming party when a mother with two daughters rang the doorbell and was welcomed into the house; the daughters were probably around ten and nine in age. One was dark-complexion, and the other was light-complexion. When they entered the room where everyone was gathered, everyone in the room started to express how beautiful the light-complexion daughter was, and the dark-complexion daughter was ignored. The mother appeared to be proud of the attention her one daughter was receiving, not objecting. I then interjected and said they were both beautiful to acknowledge the other daughter, who looked at me with a shy smile as to say about time someone noticed me.

Another example is when I was in my early thirties, I took my girlfriend to visit a close relative of mine for the weekend. We had a wonderful visit, but before we were about to leave, my relative pulled me to the side and said, "You should not marry or have kids with her because she is too dark." Not to mention, my relative and I have dark complexions.

Also, it is common in the Black community as a collective to limit the amount of time in the sun for fear of getting darker. These insecurities stem from the standards of beauty set by the social structure of white superiority. As a collective, the Black community needs to eradicate this thinking from the psyche and stop yielding to the belief that your beautiful melanated skin is unattractive. The sun provides many health benefits, and among them is its role in supporting adequate vitamin D levels, which in turn helps boost the immune system.

This learned behavior starts early and continues to be passed from generation to generation. During the adolescent stage in the Black community, the light-skinned girls get most of the attention from the young boys, which causes the darker-skinned girls to resent/bully the light-skinned girls because most of the popular boys are chasing after the lighter-skinned girls. And in most cases, it is not that lighter-skinned girls are more attractive. It is largely because of lighter skin. Even Black entertainers, specifically in the genre of rap lyrics, express the desire for redbone/light skin women.

Black Americans, as a collective, profess to despise the treatment of discrimination based on skin color, yet as a collective, we have internalized this behavior amongst ourselves and seldom talk about it or fail to notice the behavior. When I have tried to have a conversation with other Black Americans about this topic, I often get the response, "it does not exist" or "personal preference."

If we want to change this sick way of being, we first need to acknowledge that we continue to let the social structure of white supremacy define us as a collective, which only endorses and continues to validate the social structure standards of beauty. We must readjust/reprogram our psyche on how we see ourselves. We cannot control the psyche of white people, but we can control our destiny by consciously shifting away from the labels of "light skin" and "dark skin" put on us. The color of our skin cannot and should not separate and divide us to take part in this useless internal discrimination.

As a collective, we are all accountable for maintaining the social structure of white supremacy. It is the central theme of all our lives, one group is a favorite with innate privileges, and all other groups have to continuously prove themselves to the social structure of white supremacy for acceptance.

We must strive to understand our past. As a collective, most of us leave school with a limited understanding of authentic Black American history. To gain this authentic knowledge, we must personally be committed to nourishing our minds with this authentic understanding. It is our responsibility to actively educate ourselves about our history and what our ancestors had to endure for the best nourishment of our authentic history.

As a collective, we have been socialized to believe one race is superior, and somehow, we have become addicted to that lie and have picked up terrible habits that we are not even aware of. As a collective, we cannot seem to move past this way of being and have now normalized all the practices of discrimination by embracing them, not realizing how all of this has been affecting the essence of our identity; hence as a collective, we have become accustomed to the scattered psyche as a part of normal behavior.

As stated in the previous chapter, we are anchored in America's framework of white supremacy; every institution in America is controlled or influenced by white supremacy. The impact of this has played a significant role in shaping the scattered psyche of the Black American communities as a collective. How we treat and perceive one another, the intense rivalry, envy, jealousy among us, and the denial of this truth is something that has made everything around us invisible in the form that is performed unconsciously by other people as well as by us.

At the same time, we struggle every day to recover our lost humanity, and the social structure has turned us into a self-hating version of ourselves. Self-hatred has consumed us and taken away our desire to clean up after ourselves. I am not making excuses, but we have been psychologically broken, and it has driven us into a state of dysfunction. We need to put more energy and time into loving ourselves and less time into trying to continuously prove ourselves to the social structure of white superiority for acceptance.

As a collective, the Black American community's priority should be to remove the psychological damage and wake our consciousness. I'm not saying we must be monolithic in thought, but be in sync with the way we think about ourselves, our people, and our community.

We continue to hope that God will intervene and right the wrongs of the ills we have suffered. Somehow, as a collective, we have misplaced the memory of the past, and we refuse to read and understand the accurate history of this country. Our ancestors left us the blueprint, but we refuse to pick up the mantle as a collective. With the continuing disregard for nourishing our minds, we are letting the efforts of our ancestors go in vain.

"Philosophers have long conceded, however, that every man has two educators: 'that which is given to him, and the other that which he gives himself. Of the two kinds, the latter is by far the more desirable. Indeed, all that is most worthy in a man he must work out and conquer for himself. It is that which constitutes our real and best

nourishment. What we are merely taught seldom nourishes the mind like that which we teach ourselves." - Dr. Carter G. Woodson, The Miseducation of the Negro.[53]

In the final analysis, I would like to add that the United States Constitution, the overwhelming focus of Christianization, industrial training of the former enslaved Black Americans, the propagation of anti-Black propaganda, anti-Black laws/policies, and the historical Supreme Court cases, subjective misinterpretation of the Constitution by the appointed Justices have all played a momentous role in shaping the psyche of this nation.

One group desired and one group undesired. It plays a pivotal role in all our lives and as a collective nation, we are complicit in it and we all have some responsibility to eradicate what has been enforced upon us.

One way of doing this is every institution of higher learning in this country should offer an accurate Afro-American history major that is not codified in white supremacy, and irrespective of a student major, in order to receive a degree, it should be mandatory for every student to enroll in an elective course that offers an accurate portrayal of Afro-American history. As Raoul Peck stated in his monumental documentary, Exterminate All the Brutes, "*The victors get to tell the story.*" This implies that history is not grounded in truth, rather it's the victor's interpretation of the truth and the false truth of history that is fed to the people. With time people start to believe, forget, and propagate the same fiction of history as the truth. That is precisely

---

[53]Woodson, Carter. G. (1990). *The Mis-Education of the Negro. First Africa World Press, Inc. First Published by The Associated Publishers (1933).*

why it holds such immense significance to comprehend and embrace accurate Black American history, practice self-love, support Black businesses, elect conscious leaders, and above all respectively challenge the institution of white supremacy.

References

Adichie, Chimamanda, N. (2014). *The danger of a single story* [Video].
TED Talks.
https://www.ted.com/talks/chimamanda_ngozi_adichie_the_dange
r_of_a_single_story/c

Alexander, Michelle. (2012). *The New Jim Crow: Mass Incarceration in
the Age of Colorblindness.* The New Press, New York.

Amendment Summary: 27 Updates to the U.S. Constitution. (n.d.-b).
https://www.u-s-history.com/pages/h926.html

Anderson, James D. *"Northern Foundations and the Shaping of Southern
Black Rural Education, 1902-1935." History of Education
Quarterly, vol. 18, no. 4, 1978, pp. 371–96. JSTOR,
https://doi.org/10.2307/367710. Accessed 3 Apr. 2022.*

Barrows, Isabel, C. (1890). *First Mohonk Conference On The Negro
Question: Held At Lake Mohonk, Ulster County, New York, June
4, 5, 6, 1890.* George H. Ellis, Printer. pp. 7-137.

Benbow, Mark E. "Birth of a Quotation: Woodrow Wilson and 'Like
Writing History with Lightning.'" *The Journal of the Gilded Age
and Progressive Era*, vol. 9, no. 4, 2010, pp. 509–
33. *JSTOR*, http://www.jstor.org/stable/20799409.

Blackmon, Douglas A. (2008). *Slavery by Another Name: The Re-
Enslavement of Black Americans from the Civil War to World War
II. Anchor Books, A Division of Random House, Inc. New York*

Bridges, Khiara, M. (n.d.). *Implicit Bias and Racial Disparities in Health
Care.*

https://www.americanbar.org/groups/crsj/publications/human_righ ts_magazine_home/the-state-of-healthcare-in-the-united-states/racial-disparities-in-health-care/

Chibelushi, Wedaeli. (2020). Who Dominates the World's Black Hair Industry? - Pride Magazine. *Pride Magazine - Celebrating the Woman of Colour.* https://www.pridemagazine.com/who-dominates-the-worlds-black-hair-industry/

Chui, Michael. Gregg, Brian. Kohli, Sajal. and Stewart, Shelly. (2021). *A $300 billion opportunity: Serving the emerging Black American consumer.* (2021, August 6). McKinsey & Company. https://www.mckinsey.com/featured-insights/diversity-and-inclusion/a-300-billion-dollar-opportunity-serving-the-emerging-black-american-consumer

Civil Rights Act of 1875. The Supreme Court. The First Hundred Years. Primary Sources – PBS. https://thirteen.org/wnet/suremecourt/antebellum/sources_docume nt7.html

Civil Rights Cases, 109 U.S. 3 (1883). (Harlan, John, M. dissent opinion) from WESTLAW

Declaration of Independence (1776)." *Bill of Rights Institute*, 4 July 1776, billofrightsinstitute.org/primary-sources/declaration-of-independence.

Degruy, Joy (PhD) (2005). *Post Traumatic Slave Syndrome: America's legacy of Enduring Injury & Healing.* Uptone Press.

Di Angelo, Robin (2018). *White Fragility: Why it's So Hard for White People to Talk About Racism. Beacon Press.*

Douglass, Frederick. (1845). "Narrative of the Life of Frederick Douglass: An American Slave, Written by Himself." The Anti-Slavery Office.

Dray, Philip (2008). Capitol Men: The Epic Story of Reconstruction Through the Lives of the First Black Congressmen. Houghton Mifflin Harcourt Publishing Company, New York.

Du Bois, W.E.B. (PhD) (2003). *The Souls of Black Folk.* Barnes & Noble Classics, New York – First published in 1903.

Exterminate All the Brutes. Directed and written by Rauol Peck. Performances by Actors Ettore d' Alessandro, Josh Hartnett, Caisa Ahlroth, Richard Brake, Aissa Maiga, Stefan Konarske, Shane Woodward, Edward Arnold, and Denis Lyons. HBO Series, (2021).

Goldberg, Barry. and Shubinski, Barbara. (2020). *Black Education and Rockefeller Philanthropy from the Jim Crow South to the Civil Rights Era - REsource.* REsource. https://resource.rockarch.org/story/black-education-and-rockefeller-philanthropy-from-the-jim-crow-south-to-the-civil-rights-era/

Hale, Kori. (2021). The $300 Billion Black American Consumerism Bag Breeds Big Business Opportunities. *Forbes.* https://www.forbes.com/sites/korihale/2021/09/17/the-300-billion-black-american-consumerism-bag-breeds-big-business-opportunities/?sh=7c976dd434fc

How dollars circulate in Black Communities, *Greenwood.* (2021). https://gogreenwood.com/how-dollars-circulate-in-black-communities/

Jackson, Reid E. *"Rise of Teacher-Training for Negroes." The Journal of Negro Education*, vol. 7, no. 4, 1938, pp. 540–47. *JSTOR*, *https://doi.org/10.2307/2291802*. *Accessed 19 Jan. 2022.*

Lemons, J. Stanley. *"Black Stereotypes as Reflected in Popular Culture, 1880-1920." American Quarterly*, vol. 29, No. 1, 1977, pp. 102–16. *JSTOR*, *https://doi.org/10.2307/2712263*. *Accessed 20 Dec. 2021.*

Letter to Horace Greeley (1862) | Lincoln's Writings. (n.d.). https://housedivided.dickinson.edu/sites/lincoln/letter-to-horace-greeley-august-22-1862/

McVean, Ada. (2019). *40 Years of Human Experimentation in America: The Tuskegee Study*. Office for Science and Society. https://www.mcgill.ca/oss/article/history/40-years-human-experimentation-america-tuskegee-study

Peeps, J.M. Stephen. "Northern Philanthropy and the Emergence of Black Higher Education---Do --Gooders, Compromisers, or Co-Conspirators?" *The Journal of Negro Education*, vol. 50, no. 3, 1981, pp. 251–69. *JSTOR*, *https://doi.org/10.2307/2295156*. *Accessed 3 Apr. 2021.*

Religion in America: U.S. Religious Data, Demographics and Statistics | Pew Research Center. (2022). Pew Research Center's Religion & Public Life Project. https://www.pewresearch.org/religion/religious-landscape-study/racial-and-ethnic-composition/

Reyes, Maritza, V. (2020). "The Disproportional Impact of COVID-19 on African Americans." Health and Human Rights, vol. 22, no. 2, pp. 299–307,

www.ncbi.nlm.nih.gov/pmc/articles/PMC7762908/#:~:text=Appro
ximately%2097.9%20out%20of%20every.

*Plessy v. Ferguson, 163 U.S. 537 (1896). (Harlan, John, M. dissent
opinion) from WESTLAW*

Rothstein, Richard. (2018). *The Color of Law: A Forgotten History of
How Our Government Segregated America.* Liveright Publishing
Corporation, New York.

Simpson, Donald. *"BLACK IMAGES IN FILM—THE 1940s TO THE
EARLY 1960s." The Black Scholar, vol. 21, No. 2, 1990, pp. 20–
29. JSTOR, http://www.jstor.org/stable/41067681. Accessed 20
Dec. 2021.*

Sixth Annual Message | The American Presidency Project. (n.d.).
https://www.presidency.ucsb.edu/documents/sixth-annual-
message

Sonmez, Felicia. (2019). McConnell says he's against reparations for
slavery: 'It would be pretty hard to figure out who to compensate.'
Washington Post.
https://www.washingtonpost.com/politics/mcconnell-says-hes-
against-reparations-for-slavery-it-would-be-pretty-hard-to-figure-
out-who-to-compensate/2019/06/18/9602330c-9205-11e9-b58a-
a6a9afaa0e3e_story.html

Spies-Gans, Paris A. (2017). "James Madison". *The Princeton & Slavery
Project. https://slavery.princeton.edu/stories/james-madison.*

"The Tradition of White Presidents at Black Colleges." *The Journal of
Blacks in Higher Education*, No. 16, 1997, pp. 93–99. *JSTOR*,
https://doi.org/10.2307/2962918. Accessed 20 Dec. 2021.

Trawalter, Sophie. (2020). *Black Americans are Systematically Under-Treated for Pain. Why?* Frank Batten School of Leadership and Public Policy | University of Virginia. https://batten.virginia.edu/about/news/black-americans-are-systematically-under-treated-pain-why

U.S. Senate: Constitution of the United States. (2021) https://www.senate.gov/civics/constitution_item/constitution.htm

University of Alabama. (2022). Students by Race/Ethnicity. Retrieved March 2, 2023, from oira.ua.edu website: https://oira.ua.edu/factbook/reports/student-enrollment/fall-term/students-by-race-ethnicity/

University of Georgia. (2022). University of Georgia | Data USA. Retrieved from datausa.io website: https://datausa.io/profile/university/university-of-georgia

Walsh, Barbara, H. (1974). *The Negro and His Education: Persuasive Strategies of Selected Speeches at the Conference for Education in the South, 1898-1914.* LSU Digital Commons. https://digitalcommons.lsu.edu/gradschool_disstheses/2769/

Washington, Reginald. (2022). *The Freedman's Savings and Trust Company and African American.* National Archives. https://www.archives.gov/publications/prologue/1997/summer/freedmans-savings-and-trust.html

Watkins, William, H. (2001). *The White Architects of Black Education: Ideology and Power in America, 1865-1954.* Teachers College Press, New York.

Woodson, Carter. G. (1990). *The Mis-Education of the Negro. First Africa World Press, Inc. First Published by The Associated Publishers (1933).*

Wright, Bobby. (PhD) (1978). *"Mentacide: The Ultimate Threat to The Black Race."* pp. 1-15.

Written by a Friend (1857), *The Experience of Thomas H. Jones, "Who Was a Slave" for Forty-Three Years.* Worcester: Printed by Henry J. Howland, No. 245 Main Street.

www.ingramcontent.com/pod-product-compliance
Lightning Source LLC
Chambersburg PA
CBHW051536120626
46551CB00012B/1251